I0149803

God's Not Dead!

True Miracle Stories of

God's Goodness and Grace

Doris Schuster

God's Not Dead!

True Miracle Stories of
God's Goodness and Grace

Doris Schuster

© 2014, Doris Schuster, CES Publishing

God's Not Dead! True Miracle Stories of God's Goodness and Grace

ISBN 978-0-9940037-0-6

Unless otherwise stated, Scripture quotations are taken from the Holy Bible, New Living Translation (NLT) copyright© 1996, 2004, 2007, 2013 by Tyndale House Foundation. Used by permission. All rights reserved.

© Doris Schuster, CES Publishing, PO Box 2126, Angus, ON, Canada, L0M 1B0 www.ChristianEditingServices.org

Book Cover Design by Quality Print, Barrie, Ontario
Cover Photography
Upper: The splendor of God
Middle: God leads us on our path towards Him
Lower Left: Prayer brings blessings
Lower Right: Trillium—the Ontario provincial flower; a beautiful symbol of the Holy Trinity—the Father, the Son and the Holy Spirit

First Edition 2014

First Printing: December 2014
Second Printing: February 2015

This book is dedicated to my sweet mother,
Johanna Boelk, who loved me, cared for me,
and taught me right from wrong,
and to my late father, Hans Boelk,
who was my first role model
as an entrepreneur and a writer.

Table of Contents

Foreword

**But my life is worth nothing to me unless I use it for
finishing the work assigned me by the Lord Jesus—the work
of telling others the Good News about the wonderful grace
of God. (Acts 20:24, NLT)**

I'd like to thank the many individuals who wrote and sent
in their stories to be published in this collection. Without them,
there wouldn't be a book! They poured out their hearts to be a
blessing to others by testifying how present God has been in
their life to work miracles. The contributors to this book are
ordinary people, living ordinary lives, but God was, and still is,
with them.

Although I had received a personal prophetic word on two
occasions that I would be publishing a book, this has been an
incredibly challenging task for me. For many years, I have felt a
deep desire to collect stories and publish a book about the
miracles that I had heard about from friends, family, and
acquaintances—stories about the wonderful works of God that
so clearly display His goodness and grace towards all of us.
Today, as I set out to finish my own story to be included in this
collection, God directed me to the Scripture quoted above.

I have a passion for telling others about all the good news I
hear. My close friends can testify to that. Many have told me
that they see the excitement in my face when I tell them God-
stories. I believe that God put the desire to publish this book in
my heart long ago and this was the year to fulfil it. At first, I
thought I would never get it done. There were so many
distractions and interruptions on a daily basis. My deadlines for
story submissions and for editing the stories were pushed

forward several times. But as the Scripture in Acts 20:24 states, "my life is worth nothing to me unless I use it for finishing the work assigned to me by the Lord Jesus."

Do you believe in signs, wonders and miracles? A recent Newsweek poll reported that 84 percent of North Americans say they believe that God performs miracles today, and 48 percent claim to have experienced or witnessed one, even in our age of widespread skepticism.

What is a miracle?

The dictionary describes a miracle as an extraordinary event or action that apparently contradicts the laws of nature and is therefore thought to be due to supernatural causes, especially to an act of God. It is a remarkable event, or a wonder. Another source describes it as an unusual or wonderful event that is believed to be caused by the power of God. We would probably all agree that a miracle is an amazing, extraordinary or unexpected event or action.

God has given us signs and wonders of all kinds throughout the ages and He hasn't stopped doing that. Reading about miracles builds our faith and gives us something to provoke our belief in a God for whom nothing is impossible. In this book, you will read some amazing true stories about miracles, including miracles of salvation, redemption, forgiveness, healing, provision, protection and even resurrection after death!

God is sovereign and He works in so many ways. Most of the time, we have no idea how He does the miracle. We just see the glorious results and we get to praise Him for that.

Sometimes He uses doctors and surgeons to heal people; sometimes He heals supernaturally. But God's plans always succeed one way or another.

This book includes dozens of miracle stories from friends and people I've never met before. Many are from my home town and the surrounding areas; some are from diverse cities and towns in other parts of Ontario. The chapters in this book are the words of the writers. Nothing has been added or taken away. However, editing and fine-tuning was carried out to correct grammar, and to make the stories more readable and enjoyable.

I know that most of us have heard about the amazing work of salvation and healing that God has been doing for decades in Africa and South Asia. But we don't often hear about local signs, wonders, and miracles in the news media. It seems that people in the Western world aren't inspired to share their God-experiences in newspapers, on the radio, or on television. Or, perhaps, the media people don't think they're worth sharing. My hope is that the readers of this book will see how active God is in the lives of people all around us. His amazing grace is available to all of us.

I'm pleased to be able to share part of my personal journey of faith and healing with you in these pages. For a couple of decades, God has been showing me great and mighty things—one step at a time. The more I see and learn, the more I want to know, for there is no end to the great works of God. My ultimate purpose in publishing my story, and all the stories of the contributors, is not to bring fame and glory to myself, but to give glory to God for all He has done for us. The writers have told their stories truthfully, and with integrity, in order to honour our God of miracles.

Many of the individuals who contributed stories to this collection wrote to me, telling me how difficult it was to write down their experiences. Some wept as they relived the details of a difficult past. Several writers admitted that they experienced additional healing as they wrote out their testimony stories for the first time. Others were thrilled to have the opportunity to share their miracles with others. Many of the writers told me that they hope their story will bring encouragement and hope to others who might be going through similar situations. Readers can have hope that if Jesus has done it once, He will do it again—for them this time. One friend put it this way: "God's power is transferred as testimonies are shared...so that the miracles replicate when they speak to someone else's heart and situation!" I love that!

I am happy to be able to share these stories with you. May they inspire you to believe in a big God who knows you and loves you. He wants to do a miracle in your life too! Perhaps your God-story will be part of my next published collection.

Many blessings!

Doris Schuster

The Faith of a Child – Ania's Story

My daughter, Ania, is a very cheerful and positive girl. She enjoys gymnastics, art and dancing. She has two sisters whom she loves very much and enjoys spending time with them. The smile and joy she has, and the energy she carries, affects everyone around her. When she was little, she could be found crying almost every night because of the nightmares she was having. She was always very frightened. Her father and I had often prayed for our daughter but the nightmares came nonetheless. One day, when Ania was four years old, she came to me, saying, "Mommy! I don't have to be scared anymore!"

"Really? What happened?" I asked her.

"I don't have to be scared because at night, Jesus came to me and said, "Ania, you don't have to be scared anymore.""

From that day on, Ania was able to sleep through the entire night without waking up or crying. These divine visits reoccurred once in a while.

In the summer of 2008, a few weeks before her eighth birthday, I took Ania shopping with me. When we were standing in line at the cash register, Ania asked if she could hold my hand. She said that she was scared she might fall due to sudden blurry vision. This had already happened a few times before.

I sensed that this could be linked to Central Auditory Processing Disorder (CAPD), a condition Ania had been diagnosed with a year before. CAPD simply meant that Ania's brain couldn't pick up impulses that her ears were sending. Therefore, she couldn't hear properly. I began to think that perhaps her brain was reacting the same way to her eyes. Soon, these incidents involving blurry vision started occurring more often—about three times a week—and were frequently accompanied by headaches. After seeking help from three different eye doctors, not even one could diagnose her. All of them had confirmed that Ania was supposed to be able to see better than she currently was. With that in mind, the last doctor sent her for an MRI examination.

Two weeks after Ania's eighth birthday, she had the MRI examination. When the results came, the pediatrician explained that Ania was diagnosed with Chiari malformation with Syringohydromyelia. At the time, I knew next to nothing about my daughter's diagnosis. Ania was referred to a pediatric neurosurgery clinic. She had to wait four months for an appointment. Those months were probably the longest months of her life. More symptoms were developing in her body and the pain wasn't limited to her head anymore. It extended to her limbs and sometimes to her entire body. The excruciating pain even woke her up during the night. There were days when the "pain killers" didn't work, so Ania had to miss school. There were also times when she could hardly move her legs and moments when she could scarcely breathe.

It was hard for her sisters, Naomi and Natalie, to watch the usually joyful Ania enduring such pain. They were trying all kinds of tricks to cheer her up. My husband, Andrew, and I were also trying to keep the atmosphere of hope and faith alive at home, but there was nothing more devastating than watching our own child suffer, knowing that we couldn't do anything to help. There were days when I started to lose faith that God will heal our daughter. I was praying for healing every day, but it seemed like my prayers weren't coming through. On such days, doubt and fear would be surrounding my mind, bringing unwanted thoughts and causing excruciating pain to my soul. However, even though my heart was filled with doubt, it seemed like God was always standing beside me.

Once, when my friend Ela called to encourage me, she said, "It is very common for people to be scared during such moments in life. Even the prophet Elijah was scared when Jezebel threatened to kill him, so he ran away. Even though he was so afraid and was hiding in the desert, the angel of the Lord came to feed him." These words of support, free of any judgment, gave me the courage to be strong again. It also helped me to realize that God was always near, despite my doubts.

Another time, when a similar crisis of faith hit me, I noticed the amazing faith in my daughters, Naomi and Ania. One day, when they were watching Christian TV, a pastor said that "God's word is like medicine for your body." Moreover, he was encouraging people to memorize one verse from the Bible instead of taking a pill, promising that, after two weeks, whoever does so will be healed from their sickness. Despite my own doubts, the girls believed in it. Ania refused to take any pain relief pills and, together with Naomi, was learning and proclaiming verses, believing that she is going to be healed. Two weeks passed and, indeed, Ania started to feel better. Even her headaches subsided. This improvement brought relief to the whole family. But this didn't last very long. The headaches started coming back and no one understood why. I wondered why my prayers were not answered. Why was the pain coming back? What could I do to help my little daughter?

In the beginning of January 2009, the time came for the long awaited doctor's appointment. A doctor specializing in neurosurgery explained the MRI images. He said that the images showed herniation of the cerebellar tonsils (known as a Chiari malformation). This basically meant that the back part of Ania's brain had slipped down and was pressing into the lower part of the rear skull, causing tremendous pain. Some other images showed extensive and severe Syringohydromyelia of the spinal cord. This meant that fluid-filled cysts had formed in the spinal cord and they were growing, pressing, and gradually damaging the nervous system. Ania's neurosurgeon said, "If this continues to progress, it may cause obstructive hydrocephalus (water on the brain) causing harmful pressure to the brain tissue, lower cranial nerve problems, as well as brain stem and spinal cord compression, which can be life threatening."

Then the doctor explained to me, in detail, how he would perform the operation and the possible risks involved, which included, but were not limited to, infection, severe bleeding, injury to neural structures resulting in significant neurological disability, stroke, and other brain problems. He also said that such an operation was necessary, since Ania had all the progressing symptoms, and he had never observed a patient improve on their own in such an advanced stage. He also suggested that it might be best for Ania to leave gymnastics, the sport she loved the most.

14

The doctor's diagnosis was distressing for me. I had to decide whether to proceed with the surgery and take the risk of possible side effects, or wait for the condition to progress and get worse. I wasn't certain which decision would be best for our little girl. Either one could end in tragedy. In the back of my mind, however, was faith in my God who heals sicknesses. So, to buy some time, I asked the doctor for another MRI examination, based on which we would make the final decision about the surgery. I also thought that if God would heal Ania, the MRI images would prove it.

We had to wait two months to get the first available MRI appointment. They were the longest two months ever. During this time, I was desperate, and I would do anything to get Ania healed by God. I preferred God's way of healing, since I was really worried that the surgery could leave serious side effects. Nevertheless, I had to make a decision. Therefore, I said before God that if Ania won't be healed by the time of the next MRI, I would have to decide on the surgery. But during those two months, I resolved that I'd do anything to see Ania healed.

When I was praying, I said, "Lord, please teach me how to pray so my prayers will be effective. Teach me how to pray, so my prayer could be answered and Ania could be healed." My husband and I decided to fast and pray for three days. At the end of the third day, we made a promise before God that if He would give Ania back to us healed, we would serve Him the way He wants us to.

A few days after this prayer, my friend, Ela, called back and said, "Sabina, there is a teacher of the Word of God, Andrew Wommack, who has amazing teachings about healing."

"I don't know Ela. I've listened to so many teachings already. Why would this be any different?" I asked.

"Well, you don't have to listen to the teachings. However, I've seen healing testimonies on Andrew Wommack's website. You have to look at those testimonies; they are amazing!" replied Ela.

Out of curiosity, I decided to watch some of the testimonial videos and was amazed at how people were praying, and how they were healed from the most terrible diseases. They didn't plea or beg God for mercy or healing. They knew that He healed them already, through Jesus Christ. So these people were thanking God for the healing and were commanding the sickness to leave, in the authority and name of Jesus Christ.

"So we can really pray like that?" I thought to myself. It was a great revelation for me. At that moment, I decided to listen to every one of Andrew's teachings on healing, miracles, Christian authority, and anything else that would benefit Ania's situation. I committed to spending many hours a day in the presence of God, listening to teachings and praying with my daughter. These teachings changed my way of thinking about righteousness, faith, spiritual laws, God's love, and other important aspects of the Christian faith.

During the period of time when Ania was waiting for her MRI appointment, she was visited a few times by Jesus and His angels at night. He talked with Ania and was telling her about her future. When I asked Ania whether she had asked Jesus why she wasn't healed yet, she answered, "Jesus said that I am healed even though I don't feel like it yet."

With this in mind, Ania and I prayed every day. We decided to ignore every doubtful thought and, instead, concentrated on Jesus' promise and the Word of God that talks about healing. We were proclaiming these promises as truth for Ania's body, and we made the decision that every symptom of disease is illegal and wrongful in Ania's body. Like the people in the testimonies, in the authority of Jesus Christ, I was commanding the pain to go away, and Ania was praising God for any progress. From then on, we began to see the results of our prayers. Whenever the pain in Ania's body would come back, we started proclaiming the Word of God and commanding the pain to leave—and it obeyed! I also ordered Ania's brain to lift up, and the fluid-filled cysts to leave Ania's spinal cord, in Jesus' name. With amazement, we noticed the pain and headaches stop occurring as frequently as before, and then they stopped completely. The blurry vision and other symptoms also disappeared. At that point, I knew in my heart that I should stop praying for healing and, instead, just thank God for it. Even though we didn't have documented evidence of recovery, we knew in our hearts that it had happened.

At the beginning of March 2009 came the day of the MRI examination and then, a week later, came the results. Ania's neurosurgeon was amazed at what the pictures showed. He had compared them with the ones made in September 2008. He explained that the cerebellar tonsils (lower part of the brain) had shifted up since the last MRI, and the fluid-filled cysts in Ania's spinal cord had decreased. The doctor was stunned! He had never seen such results in his entire career. He monitored Ania for the next two years, conducting MRI scans every six months. With each progressive scan, the doctor could see that the cysts had eventually disappeared completely and the cerebellar tonsils had lifted to the proper level. The doctor admitted to us that this was a miracle and he hadn't seen anything like it before.

Ania also had the Central Auditory Processing test to check her hearing. These results were just as amazing. Ania could now hear properly! God had made our family whole and well. She now dedicates herself to dance and has already won a few gold medals during competitions. This is the miracle that our family will never stop thanking God for and we will never forget what He has done for us.

I'd like to express a special thanks to all our friends who have supported us through prayer when we needed them most.

Some of the healing verses that helped us:

1 Peter 2:24

Isaiah 53:4-5

Psalm 103:3 and 10-11

Psalm 91

Psalm 107:20

Sabina Yurkov, Hamilton, Ontario

A Heavenly Crossing Guard

The stove timer went off, interrupting my concentrated stare at the computer screen. My little ones would soon be waiting for me to direct them across Kerr Street, as I did every day. With my guidance, they had successfully crossed this particular street dozens of times.

Yes, I could've gone down and guided them firmly by the hand from one side to the other, as I had done for the first couple of years, but I was trying so hard to move away from "smothering" and towards "mothering".

So I leaned over our 3rd floor balcony and waved, my face lighting up at the very sight of them.

Ashlea, a precocious eight year old, so full of questions, so full of life, was holding tightly to her nine-year-old brother's hand, as she had been taught to do.

Kelsea, somewhat shy but always thinking, adjusted his back pack and looked up at me expectantly. I knew he was wondering what yummy snack awaited him.

Traffic whizzed by in both directions, building as it always did at this time of day. I held my hand out flat towards them and yelled, "Wait!"

Kels took a step forward. I yelled, "Stop" and pushed my hand further in front of me, as if by doing so, I could push him back. He took another step and was now on the curb, the end of

19

his little runners protruding over the edge. He no longer held his sisters hand.

I continued to yell, "Wait" and "Stop" but, at that moment, I realized they couldn't hear me, for hurtling like a missile up the street was the number 17 Kerr Street bus.

I looked towards the intersection at the top of the street. The light was green. The bus continued to accelerate. I looked at my son, now wobbling on the curb, and quietly pleaded, "Jesus, help him."

The next few moments passed in slow motion. I watched in blurred frames, as my son began to teeter on the curb, using his arms like helicopter blades to try to steady himself. But anyone could see what was about to happen. He was losing his balance and it seemed inevitable that he would fall directly into the path of the oncoming bus!

I don't think I consciously closed my eyes. Instead, my unconscious mind decided for me. It would not let me see this most horrible thing. My eyes closed involuntarily and I choked back a scream in favour of another, not so silent plea, "JESUS, PLEASE; GOD, PLEASE!"

The bus hurtled past and I dared to open my eyes. It took me a moment to understand what I was seeing. Ashlea stood firmly planted and Kelsea was lying on the grass behind her. Not lifeless—not even slightly broken. Just half lying, half sitting, with a stunned look on his face.

Screaming at them one more time to stay where they were, I took the steps two at a time, bounding like a lioness towards her cubs.

Pulling Ashlea onto the grass, I quickly examined every inch of my son's body for signs of trauma, but there was nothing. I began to cry, letting out great heaving sobs of relief and thankfulness. Ashlea too was crying and I pulled the two of them close, thanking her over and over again for saving her brother's life.

A couple of minutes later, we were on our feet, hands tightly clenched, when Ashlea said, "Mommy?"

"Yes honey?" I replied, concentrating on the cars coming towards us in both directions.

"I don't know what happened. I don't think I did anything. I think it was the big man who was with us."

Yet there was no man to be seen. I was sure that my little ones had been miraculously protected by an angel.

Gloria Lawrenson, Wasaga Beach, Ontario

One Blessing After Another

Our First Home

As is the case with many people, one of our dreams as a young couple was to be able to buy our own home. This dream became possible in the fall of 1976, in New Brunswick. My husband and I were both working full time. We had a small down payment and decided to take the plunge and buy a new home in a developing subdivision. We were thrilled with being able to choose our own colours, carpet, etc.

After living in our new home for one year, we both accepted the Lord as our personal Saviour. Through different circumstances, we met a Christian who invited us to a crusade and ultimately we made a decision to follow the Lord. We were open to the leading of the Lord in our lives and, in 1977, my husband began to feel the Lord calling him to Bible College, not necessarily knowing it would lead to full time ministry. We made up our minds to go if he was accepted at the college. Soon the news came that he was accepted!

As much as we really loved our new house, we were willing to go where the Lord wanted us to go. We prepared to move to Bible College, in Ontario, in September 1977. When we tried to sell our house, several people were interested, but each time the deal would fall through. Eventually, perhaps a month before we were to leave, we put an ad in the local newspaper to rent it. We were getting worried, knowing that we couldn't continue to pay a mortgage in New Brunswick and pay the rent for a house in Ontario.

Already we were taking a step of faith, since my husband would be studying full time and would not be earning an income. We had a 3-month old baby and I would be looking for work to support the family.

The moving truck was arriving that Saturday morning. The week before our planned move, the house was still not rented or sold. We felt that the Lord was calling us to go and, whether or not the house was rented, we would be obedient and go. We felt a bit like Abraham, but were willing to take the step. On Wednesday, a man phoned and said he saw a "For Rent" sign in the window of the living room of our house. He came over on Thursday night and signed the papers on the spot to rent the house. Not a minute too soon…

Saturday morning, the U-Haul truck was packed and we left on one of our many adventures. Though we were stressed a bit, God came through for us. Perhaps He was testing our faith, but God is always on time, never late.

On the Road Again

Being in the ministry can be a very "moving" experience, if you know what I mean. After completing Bible College in 1980, my husband was offered a position as Assistant Pastor in an Ontario church. He would be assisting the late Art Ettinger, our first Pastor—the one who had led us to accept Jesus as the

Lord of our lives. After two years of growing closer to the Lord in the church we were attending, and then studying for three years at college, we found ourselves starting to work in full-time ministry.

It was moving day again and my husband was driving the U-Haul (and this wasn't his last time either). Our 3-year-old was in the truck with him and I was following behind in our station wagon with our 6-week-old baby in his car bed in the back seat. This was before the days of baby car seats. Our move was approximately a three hour drive. It was the month of May, a clear day, and the baby was sleeping...no sweat! We had worked out a plan that, if I had to stop, I'd flash my lights and put on my blinkers and he would know to pull over.

We were driving along Highway 401 uneventfully when, suddenly, a flatbed trailer passed me in the passing lane and lost a piece of his cargo. His cargo consisted of huge, jagged pieces of scrap metal that were tied down with chains. It happened when his vehicle was just a few car lengths ahead of me. Suddenly, this piece of metal bounced once in the middle of the lane, bounced again up into the air, and then landed right in front of my car. I had no choice but to run over it and heard it scraping all the way under the car. It all happened so fast that I had no warning to be able to pull over or stop. It wouldn't have been wise to slam on the brakes or swerve either, even if I'd had enough time.

When I was able to, I did pull over and so did a tractor trailer driver behind me who saw what had happened. Seeing the danger of leaving this large piece of metal in the middle of the road, he tried to pull it off. He struggled, but managed to drag it over to the side of the road. Unfortunately, however, other cars behind me couldn't avoid it or stop in time and ran over it, some blowing their tires. The tractor trailer man radioed ahead to ask if anyone had felt a shift in their load or noticed that they lost something.

Even though I was still feeling quite shaken, I knew I had to catch up to my husband, Fernand, who was surely wondering where I had disappeared to. He had noticed that I was no longer following and had pulled over to wait for me. When I caught up to him, I told him the whole story and we proceeded to report the incident to the nearest police station. We finally continued on to our destination. The front bumper and a section under the car were damaged. It was approximately $1,200 in repairs that we couldn't afford, but our insurance covered it.

The Lord's hand of protection was amazing that moving day. One second difference in timing would have put that piece of metal bouncing up off the road through my windshield, possibly killing me and my baby son, rather than hitting the pavement and going under the car. I wouldn't have been here to tell the story of this move…

North to Quebec

Our next move was to a town way up north in Quebec. A strange incident occurred while we were pastoring in Chibougamau, between April 1982 and August 1984. It happened in the dead of winter, during the month of February, when the temperature was minus 35 degrees. Six weeks of -30 to -35 degree weather was normal for Chibougamau! We were living in the parsonage of the church.

One night, around 3:00 a.m., someone was banging on our back door and yelling loudly. My husband and I awoke with a start and, after some hesitation, I went down to the kitchen, to the back door, to ask who it was and what they wanted? The man cried out, "Feu, feu!!" which means **FIRE** in French. Looking out the kitchen window towards the church, I saw that the shed that was attached to the church was, indeed, on FIRE! The shed was where we stored the wood and the buckets of hot cinders. We heated the church and parsonage with wood furnaces.

Even after seeing the shed on fire, it was strange that I still didn't open the door—almost as though I wasn't supposed to see the man's face. I assured the man that my husband would come right out. Fernand dressed quickly and went out to find the man busily throwing snow on the fire. Fernand and the man were so preoccupied with shoveling snow on the fire that they were not even talking to one another.

After 15 to 20 minutes, the fire was under control and not much of the shed was even damaged very badly. It had been caught in time. The shed was only about 20 feet from the house and could have caused a major fire, consuming both the church and the parsonage, had we not been warned in the night. When Fernand turned to thank the man and find out why he was out there walking at 3:00 in the morning, in -35 degree weather, he was gone. He never noticed him leaving either. The man didn't say goodbye, or anything else for that matter. I'm sure that, under normal circumstances, a "hero" or "Good Samaritan" would have waited to tell his story of how he noticed the fire, and stayed to talk for a few brief minutes.

Fernand never even had the chance to thank him. I knew right away that it was an angel. I mean, who walks around in Chibougamau, in the middle of the night, in those freezing temperatures? The people in our church were mostly employed by the three gold mines or the two saw mills that were located just outside of our town. I later asked some of them what time the shifts finished, in case it could have been a worker from the mines or the saw mills. But the times didn't coincide. In a small town of 5,000 people, surely someone would have talked about the fire the next day and we would have found out who the "Good Samaritan" was. But we never did! I'm convinced to this day that it was, indeed, an angel who helped us put out the fire that night. If only I had opened the door…!

Sowing in Quebec and Reaping in Ontario

After another move, we ended up pastoring in Quebec City. As life has its ups and downs, even for Christians, our time pastoring in Quebec was not a prosperous time for our family financially. We found ourselves coming to the end of the lease of our only car. Because we had driven more kilometers than were allowed in the contract, we had to pay a large sum of money just to finish the lease contract. We weren't in any financial position to secure a loan for another car, even an older one.

Miraculously, my father offered to give us his old 1989 Mercury Marquis. He had driven it to Florida with the intention of leaving it there and using it while spending the winters in the south. This would mean that my father and mother would no longer have to drive down to Florida; they would be able to fly back and forth instead. It was a sacrifice for my dad; even though his health was good, he was approaching his eighties.

It was all arranged. My sister paid to fly him down to Florida and he drove the car back. It was early September, but the temperature was still in the 90s. On his way home to Ontario, he encountered a little misfortune. He had to stop to have a minor repair done to the car and then he was off on his way again. A few hundred miles later, it began to rain.

That's when he discovered that the mechanic had done something wrong and his power windows no longer worked. Can you picture this poor old man driving through a terrible downpour in South Carolina, unable to put the windows up? People were passing and honking at him, making signs to put up the windows, as if he wouldn't have done so if he could have! My poor dad! This was very embarrassing for a proud man.

In any case, he arrived back in Canada and I travelled to Ontario to drive the car back to Quebec. It really was a blessing when we needed it. We wondered whether we had done something to deserve this blessing. Did this happen because of my faithfulness or the faithfulness of my husband? I don't think so and here's why.

One day, in September, my youngest son, David, who was 16 at the time, asked me for some money to go to an activity. To any parent this would not be considered unusual behaviour for a teenager. However, his request seemed strange to me, considering that he had just finished working for the summer, fixing computers for the Quebec School Board. He was starting college in the fall, in Quebec City. He had always been independent and responsible for his age. I couldn't figure out why he was asking for money when he had worked and saved all summer. When I asked him, he was hesitant and avoided the question, but after my insisting, the story came out. He told me that he had given it all to the church...*all* of his summer earnings! I couldn't believe my ears. I knew that he was not stingy and I also knew that he was tithing, but all of it? Our teenage son said that he felt God was telling him to give it all; so he did. My heart just dropped. I was so proud that he would be so obedient and trusted God to provide. Our children put us to shame sometimes.

Suddenly, it hit me like a ton of bricks. David had been obedient to God to give that money to the church and the Lord spoke to my dad to give us the car. The Lord really showed me, in my heart, that it was because of my son's financial faithfulness that we were blessed with the car. I shared that with my son and he said, jokingly, something to the effect of, "Oh, I thought *I* would get blessed..."

The following spring, after graduating from CEGEP (which is college in Quebec), David was accepted to the University of Waterloo in Ontario, which was known to be the most prominent university for the field he was entering—Math and Computer Science. Just to be accepted at this university was an honour. He was also accepted into the Co-op Program, which allows the student to work and study alternately, enabling the student to pay for a large portion of their studies as they go. This was, in itself, an answer to prayer!

Along with his acceptance came another special blessing. Because of his academic achievement, he was awarded a $9,000 scholarship towards his four years of study! I believe the Lord didn't forget about the day our son offered up his summer earnings, never expecting this blessing from the "Master of Multiplication".

Barbara Landry, Innisfil, Ontario

Dreams Do Come True

As a child, growing up in a large family, on a dairy farm in southern Ontario, all I wanted when I grew up was to get married and have a family of my own. I couldn't imagine anything better than to have my own child to love and care for.

I fell in love and married just after my 23rd birthday. It was the happiest day of my life up to that time. I was looking forward to setting up a home and establishing a family of my own.

You can surely imagine the disappointment, the devastation, the questions, and the discouragement that followed as, month after month, year after year after year after year, there was no baby. Why couldn't we get pregnant? My friends were having babies; multiple babies!!! I was happy for them, but that became increasingly difficult. In my pain and confusion, I began crying out to God. I wanted a child. I longed for a child, especially a baby girl.

Around the fifth year of our marriage, people started making comments to me, like, "Isn't it time to start a family?" I would cry inside. That's when I made a decision. I'm not going to make light of a situation that is tearing me apart inside. So I would tell people the truth. I would say something like, "We would if we could." End of conversation. People usually didn't know what to say after that.

Many days I would pour out my aching heart to the Lord. I would cry out to Him about my desire for a child. The answer always seemed to be, "It's not the right time." I often wondered when the right time would be and I know that, at least on one occasion, I screamed back at Him, "When will it be time?" I remember praying at one point that, if it wasn't His will for us to have children, that He would take the desire from me. The desire never left but seemed to become even stronger!! Those were extremely difficult years.

At times, I would almost lose complete hope. Yet a flicker of hope always remained alive, somewhere deep inside me. I could not give up completely. Occasionally I would read the Old Testament stories of women who also deeply desired a child. I could identify with their struggles. They waited many long years for God to fulfill their desires. But God always did answer the cries of their hearts and blessed them with a child. Their stories gave me hope and I wanted the same kind of faith in God that they had.

What I haven't mentioned is that I was carrying a lot of emotional pain from my childhood and I was experiencing numerous physical ailments that seemed untreatable. I was a mess! But God, in His grace and His mercy, brought my husband and me into fellowship with a wonderful, caring small group. Week after week, they loved on me and ministered to me. I began to feel safe with them and to share my pain with them. I grew closer to the Lord. Healing was beginning.

In the summer of 1990, my husband and I attended a meeting at our church. After the meeting, we were sitting and talking with Gary and Winona, the leaders of our small group. They began to pray for me, and my husband asked the Lord to give me a sign of His love for me. Immediately B-A-B-Y flashed across the screen of my mind, quickly followed by the question, how do I know that was from God and not my own selfish desire? I remember thinking, "I can't tell anyone this." Then Gary began to chuckle and said something like, "this shall be a sign to you; you shall see a baby..." I can't remember exactly what his words were, but I was astounded! God had just confirmed His word to me through someone else! So I shared what had happened to me. Together, the four of us claimed that word as a promise that God would give us a child. My faith level soared, and I trusted God to fulfill that promise like I'd never trusted Him before.

A little while later, I was prayed for by an elderly gentleman, who was known to pray for infertile couples, and they would become pregnant and have a child. Guess what? A couple of months later, I was thrilled to discover that I was, indeed, with child! I was thrilled! I wanted to stand on a mountaintop and shout it out to the world! Family and friends rejoiced with us.

Then the bleeding began. I spent five days on complete bed rest, hoping and praying the bleeding would stop. We needed a miracle. During the days of uncertainty, I poured out my fear and confusion to the Lord, and asked Him to speak to me. He responded with the words, "Nothing is impossible with Me." I wasn't sure what that meant for my situation at the time, but I kept His words in my heart. On February 15, 1991, we lost our baby. I was stunned! That night, I had a vivid dream. I saw Jesus, holding in His arms a bundle wrapped in a light blue and green checkered blanket, and I knew, without a doubt, that He was holding my baby, my son. At first I responded to that picture with anger, as I felt robbed. But later on it became a comfort to me and it is now a precious picture that I will never forget. I look forward to meeting my son, Michael Steven, in heaven someday. I believe God gave me his name as it was stuck in my mind and heart from the time I knew I was pregnant.

The following months we worked through the grieving process, but I wasn't sure if God could be trusted after all that. Why would He promise me a baby, only to take it from me? Yet somehow I knew that there really wasn't anywhere else to turn but to the Lord. I learned a lot through the experience. I experienced God's grace in such a way that, for the first time in my life, I began to understand what grace really was. The experience seemed to open the door to my innermost being, and God began revealing, touching, and healing deep hidden areas of my life. 1991 was a difficult year, but the growth, the healing, and the love I experienced made it all worthwhile.

Sometime after the miscarriage, I began to trust God again for a baby. I looked up Luke 1:37 in the Amplified Bible and read, "For with God nothing is ever impossible and no word from God shall be without power or impossible of fulfillment." Those words blessed me, and I clung to them.

In February 1992, I discovered that I was pregnant again. God was faithful to His word. We were excited and, from the moment we knew another child was on the way, it felt so right. Oh how I loved being pregnant! I clearly remember Mother's day that year. We hadn't told people yet about the pregnancy. But, that day, the pastor asked all the mothers and mothers-to-be to stand up. What do I do? Finally I stood up and, as I did, the people around me began to clap. Yes, clap! It was an awesome moment. I received my first carnation as a mother that day.

God was so good to me! I had a wonderful, enjoyable pregnancy. I felt soooo blessed! In the early morning hours, on a cold October night, in 1992, in the comfort of our home, our baby girl came into the world. At my first glimpse of her, I couldn't help but cry out, "Oh God!" She was the most beautiful baby I had ever seen! So perfect in every way! I was overwhelmed! What a blessing! What a gift! We named her Shannon Rose because, according to our baby name book, Shannon means "God's gift" and Rose means "symbol of love." She definitely was a gift from God and a very real sign of His love to me.

Through the years, we have enjoyed every stage of Shannon's life. We are so proud of the young woman that she has become and I have been so blessed to be her mother. Now a young man has entered her life and stolen her heart, and wedding plans are underway. I look forward to holding grandchildren someday, as God's promise to me continues to the next generation. Blessed be the name of the Lord!

Carol Weber, Moorefield, Ontario

The Hound of Heaven

I'd like to share a couple of experiences of how active God can be to get your attention.

I was almost killed in a car accident during a blinding blizzard in the winter of 80/81. Our family went out to dinner at the Village Inn, in Thornton, Ontario. While driving on the 8th Line of Innisfil Township, my car ended up in the ditch as I moved to the right to avoid the oncoming traffic. My dad and I were in the car and my wife, sister and brother-in-law in a car behind us. Dad and I got out of my car and walked to a farm house to call for a tow truck. As we were walking back to my car, we saw another car coming, busting through the snow drifts. Suddenly, it lost control and was heading straight for us. Dad jumped into the ditch but I couldn't make the leap since I was knee deep in snow. The thought rushed through my mind...*I'm about to be run over, on a snow blown road no less*...but I wasn't ready to die! I flopped into the snow next to the ditch and awaited my fate. But nothing happened. As I looked up, I saw the car plough into the ditch across the road. The driver jumped out of the car and ran towards me.

We observed that his car had missed my legs by less than 12 inches. Upon close examination of the scene, it appeared that the only thing that had kept the car from going into the ditch and crushing me was a small patch of very "green" grass that the front right tire passed over.

My aunt later told me, "Someone upstairs likes you." But who was that anyway? I didn't really believe in God.

For a number of years, I was an avid sailor and, in the summer of 1981, I lost my wallet overboard while sailing Kempenfelt Bay. It was my common practice to stow away my personal effects in the storage compartment of my Cygnus day sailor. The winds were brisk and I needed to be ready should I have to do some hiking in the heavier winds. Hiking is the action of moving your body weight as far to windward side (upwind) as possible, in order to decrease the extent the boat heels (leans away from the wind). To achieve this, you sit on the gunnels (the rail that surrounds the edge of the boat) and stretch out as far as possible, to keep the boat upright. The weather conditions that day were perfect for a single tack to Big Bay Point (some eight to nine miles away) and then back again. What a ride!

Once we got back to the Barrie marina, I noticed my wallet was missing! Since I forgot to stow my wallet, I concluded that it popped out of my back pocket somewhere up the bay. I uttered a quick prayer to God, "Please God, bring back my wallet and I'll go to church on Sunday." Well, you guessed it! My wife, Marliene, received a call from the Barrie Police about two weeks later. Someone had turned in my wallet! Wow, that shook me up! When I picked up the wallet, the police officer gave me the name and phone number of the people who found it. Apparently its discovery was very unusual. I called and the woman who answered the phone shared that she and her husband were boating in a small runabout down Kempenfelt Bay, and her husband had an urge to go beachcombing. They beached their boat at Tollendale Park, the husband stepped out of the boat and found my wallet within a few feet of their location!

That experience shook me up; God had my attention…Marliene and I started to attend a small Anglican church, in St. Paul, Ontario, shortly afterwards.

I ultimately surrendered my life to Jesus Christ after discussing a number of these weird occurrences with my Pentecostal brother-in-law and reading the book, The Late Great Planet Earth. After praying for Jesus to come into my life, I dared God to change me. It's at that point that my life really began to change for the better!

Brian Cathline, Barrie, Ontario

I Am Free!

My story is about emotional healing and transformation. If truth be told, it's a story of how a girl who was once dead was brought back to life.

I was born a month early, on the way to the hospital, coming out breach. I often think how the enemy is the thief who comes to kill, steal and destroy, and I can look back at times in my life where he has tried to do that, even from my birth. But God has always had a plan for my life—a plan to prosper me and not to harm me. I've learned that the saying "Greater is He who is in me than he who is in the world" is true.

My mother and father have their own stories to tell, but I can share just a little of what I know because it does impact my life in a big way. My dad didn't want to marry my mom, but he did because she was with child—my brother. My dad, like so many dads before him, married because he thought it was the right thing to do. I've never believed that getting married to someone you didn't love was the right thing to do, but how many of us do it? "If I speak in the tongues of men or of angels, but do not have love, I am only a resounding gong or a clanging cymbal." (1 Corinthians 13:1, NIV) My dad didn't want more children. I don't think he even wanted my brother; it just happened, so he dealt with it. My mom, knowing my dad didn't love her and so desperately wanting to be loved, also knew that my dad was on his way out. So she got pregnant with me... I was supposed to save their marriage. That's a heavy load for an unborn child to carry.

So it began, right from the start. I was born into the world feeling unloved, unwanted, and with a purpose that, in no way, was mine to fulfill. There were lots of fights between my mom and dad in the first two years of my life, and I guess it didn't help that I was a colicky baby. Maybe I could feel the tension around me; who knows?

Then my dad left. Not only did he leave my mom, but he left my brother and me—never to return—no birthday cards, no phone calls, no Christmas visits. Nothing...he was gone! I had already failed and, for some reason, I felt it. I did not fulfill my purpose. I didn't save their marriage. I was a failure! That was a lie but I believed it, even at such a young age. The thief will come in the night, and that night was my childhood. So far, at the age of two, these were the lies I believed: I wasn't wanted, wasn't loved, was a failure, wasn't good enough. No wonder I got sick; so sick that they didn't know what was wrong with me. They did exploratory surgery on me to find out my bowels had tied in a knot. I was all twisted up, and no wonder, since I believed all those lies.

The surgery left me with a big ugly scar on my stomach, which made me believe I was damaged goods. This brings me to about three—almost four years of age. With my dad gone and my mom always so sad and drinking all the time, starving for attention, longing for love and approval, it made me an easy target for the other broken and sick people in this world. And it didn't take long for them to find me when my mom was too drunk to take care of me.

So the abuse started. Sexual abuse never begins at the point of the first sexual contact. "It begins in the matrix of some level of emotional neglect, role distortion, harshness, coldness, rigidity, and fear-induced loyalty. In most cases, the family, prior to the abuse, was a festering sore where disease and emptiness were a normal part of life." (from *The Wounded Heart: Hope for Adult Victims of Childhood Sexual Abuse*, Dr. Dan B. Allender, page 107). Shame then entered my life. Mainly for being a child from a divorced home and because, back 40 years ago, it was a rare thing having a mother who drank. Secondly, because I was a child who was damaged emotionally, physically and mentally. What a start! But wait, there's still more.

We moved from our family home—from my tree house which my dad had built, and my sandbox where I spent most of my time. I remember that I was only four years old at this time. We lived in a small village and that's all I had ever known. I didn't want to move. How would dad ever find us? I remember crying and screaming, "No we can't move; dad won't find us." Even to this day, the memory of moving still fills me with sorrow, for it's the day hopelessness entered my life. I wanted so much for my dad to come home and to save us from all the bad things that were happening, to make mommy happy again, and to stop the bad men from coming around. I thought, "Where are you, daddy, and why do you not love me anymore?" It must be true that I'm not loveable...nobody loves me. The men who were abusing me would say, "You're a bad girl," and I believed them. They all must have been right.

We moved to a bigger city. There were all new people around—a new start. Maybe now mommy would be happy.

Maybe now daddy would come home. Maybe now these men would stop coming by. But no such luck. My mom drank more, took us out with her more, and had more people over because she was lonely. At one time, my mom had known the Lord and served the Lord as a Salvation Army Officer. I had seen the pictures. She would tell me about Jesus and God—tell me of their love for us. She would teach me songs of praise and, when she was drunk, she would get me to sing them to her friends..."Amazing grace, how sweet the sound," and "Jesus said, 'Come to the water, stand by my side...'" I would talk to this God that she told me about and ask Him for help. I would ask Him to save my mom, and to heal her of her drinking problem. She also taught me the song "Jesus loves me; this I know..." and I would sing this song over and over again and wonder why He didn't love me. Was it because nobody loved me? Or because people touched me and I was now dirty? Or was God like my father, who was there, living far away, but didn't want anything to do with us? I did believe that there was a God but He didn't want me. This was the ultimate lie. God doesn't love me. If He did love me, why did He let these bad things happen to me, my mom, and my brother? Couldn't He hear me? Did He not hear my mom every night, as she lay in bed, crying, "God where are you? Help me!" Did He not hear us?

One night, when I was six, my mom got so drunk that she was always on the phone. She would call everyone. I used to wish that I had a phone so she would call me and talk to me. She called the Children's Aid Society to come and get me and my brother, and then she passed out. I woke up to my mother screaming. I was terrified. I had never heard her scream like that before. I had heard her scream for lots of reasons before, but never like that. Fear entered my life, like never before. Two men entered my room and told me to come with them. I had no idea what was happening. I could still hear my mom screaming and yelling. I could hear men's voices yelling back. I did not want to leave my room, but they were telling me to hurry up, that everything was going to be OK. Yeah right…for whom? As we got to the top of the stairs, I saw my mom being held down by two police officers. She broke free from one of them and punched him right in the face. He punched her right back! All respect that I may have had for men, or anyone in authority, went right out the window at that moment. Anger filled my heart, along with the fear.

Out the door we went—my brother and I. We were taken to what they call a relief home. They were expecting only one child—my brother—but because they had nowhere for me, they had to keep me too. This reinforced the "nobody wants me" feeling that I had.

This was the first of 15 different homes for me. My mom would stop drinking and win us back home. Then she would drink again, or try to kill herself, and my brother or I would find her with pills and beer bottles all around her, and we would phone for help. We knew never to bring anyone home with us because we never knew what we would come home to. There could be someone with our mother who was passed out on the couch, or she could be drunk on the front porch, yelling at the neighbours. We never knew. Sometimes it was worse to find her not drinking, because she was so angry, so distant, and so sad. Sometimes I would want her to be drinking because she would be happier, at first. So in and out of foster homes I went—at first with my brother—but then he got to stay with my grandma. Not me though.

At seven, I got really sick again. This time, I ended up in the hospital for almost a year with rheumatic fever. Many times no one came to visit me because of the court cases with Children's Aid or my mom's drinking. I would see other kids in the rooms receive gifts, have lots of visitors, and get lots of love. It made me resentful and bitter. I was left with a heart murmur and arthritis in all my joints. I think that's what happens when you hold on to bitterness and resentments.

One time, my aunt took me from one of the homes that I lived in and took me out of the country, and left me there. It's too much to relive. That was how I began my life. And there's lots left out...there's lots more to tell. There was so much brokenness, and from this brokenness I made choices that affected my whole life. I never let anyone in because I didn't want to be hurt. I gave my life to Jesus as a child; then I would not let Him in for fear that He would reject me, just like I had been rejected so much in my childhood. I so wanted to be loved, but fear keep me from ever letting anyone really love me—even my husband. I've been with him since I was 15, but I chose someone who really couldn't give me what I needed or wanted. I died to longings long before I even knew what longings were. "In the midst of shame, longing for what the heart craves intensifies the anguish of the soul... For the woman who has been abused, one of the greatest enemies of the soul is the longing for intimacy." (*The Wounded Heart*, Dan B. Allender)

I tried to fill this hole in my heart with people, sex, drugs, drinking, getting married, having kids, food. I think I tried everything and nothing could fill this empty space in my life. In my heart, at 33 years old, I wanted to die. I was a wife to one, a mother to four, an alcoholic, and a drug addict. I was addicted to prescription pills, but crystal meth had become my drug of choice and it was taking me down fast. I hated who I had become and what I was doing to my children. But I didn't know where to turn. I had tried everything I knew on my own and nothing worked. No one could help, although many tried.

My marriage was also a mess. There was a lot of abuse there too. I just didn't care anymore about life. I had lost my mother to alcohol years earlier and I remembered singing to her as she lay dying in the hospital, "Amazing grace, how sweet the sound…" and "Jesus said, 'Come to the water, stand by my side…'"

I had sent my kids to Power Force, which was a kids club that the church put on, and I had told them about Jesus and God, like my mother had done for me. But where was He? I prayed for death—for God to let me die.

I ended up in a shelter with nothing but the clothes on my back. I had lost everything, or should I say I walked away from everything. I thought my life would never turn around. That night, as I lay in the bed at the shelter, seeing what people on meth would call "shadow people" standing all around my bed, or demons, I cried out, "God, help me!" and then went to sleep. I woke up in the morning feeling better than I had in years, not yet realizing that God had helped me. Not long after that, I returned home to my family, saying I would get help for my drinking if my husband would get help for his anger. I said I would go to ask for help but, if anyone talked to me about God, I would hit them. Then a funny thing happened. God started hitting me everywhere I went! At the AA meetings through people's stories, and through people that He put in my path, God started talking with me!

The cravings for alcohol left and that was a miracle. The obsession to use meth was also gone. There was no urge to take pills anymore. That cloud of sadness was dissipating.

One day, my daughter came home from the church group with a little note that said, "Come try Sunday School." She wanted to go. So, that Sunday, we went to church. Ever since that day, I've been warning people that the Pentecostal church has greeters at the front door. Later I realized that it's a good thing that they do because the greeters that Sunday are the reason that I ended up staying at the church. If it hadn't been for that friendly couple at the door, I would have just dropped my daughter off and left. But they were so nice—talking to me and asking me questions. During that conversation, the Holy Spirit was working not only on me, but also on the pastor inside the sanctuary, to find some way to get me to stay.

While the greeters were talking to me, the doors to the sanctuary were opened and a Bible study was going on. The pastor said something about how our Prime Minister had ruined our country and, at that point, something rose up inside of me. I asked if I could go in there. They said, "yes," so away I went, with all intentions to give this pastor a piece of my mind because I happened to like our Prime Minister.

I can't tell you what happened next but the church was filled with people. My daughter was beside me and asked if we could stay. I was too embarrassed to leave, so we stayed. The kids were eventually dismissed to go to their Sunday School classes and the music started. People started singing. I was wondering how the heck I could get out of there when, all of a sudden, the minister said, "Sorry folks; we're going to start again." Then he said, "I feel the Lord wants us to sing number 45," and they started singing, "Amazing grace, how sweet the sound..." The tears came down my cheeks. Some lady came and sat beside me with a box of Kleenex, but she didn't say a word. She just sat with me, which meant the world to me. This said to me, "You're wanted, I see you, and I care," without saying a single word out loud. Next thing I knew, the pastor said, "Sorry folks; we are not going to follow the program. Today the Lord wants someone here to know that they have been carrying baggage around their whole life and they don't have to carry it around any longer. Jesus died to take it all away. You can leave that baggage here today." Then he told everyone to bow their head. I thought, "Who is going to listen to this guy?" But, to my surprise, everyone did bow their head! I seemed to be the only one looking around. He said, "If this is you, and you want to leave that baggage here today, at Jesus' feet, you can do that. If you would like to rededicate your life to the Lord, raise your hand and I will pray for you." I raised my hand and the minister prayed for me.

My life hasn't been the same since then. I once was dead but now I live! I was blind but know I see! My Lord, my God, has never left me. He's been with me all along. He has restored to me all that the locust (the devil) has taken from me. I am free from all the lies that the enemy has been telling me. I am set free from the bondages of addiction to drugs, alcohol and pills. I am healed of the arthritis in my legs and there is no trace of a heart murmur. Instead of doom and gloom, I can now spread the

Good News. What Jesus did for me, He can, and will do for you. He whom Jesus sets free is free indeed, and I am free indeed. Expect a miracle! Even if you don't, you might still get one.

Julie Pugliese, Mount Forest, Ontario

He Healed All My Diseases

I have experienced many, many miracles over the course of being on this planet for 50 years. The following are some of the highlights:

When I was a young girl, I was riding my tricycle down a steep hill. Being unable to stop, an angel intervened and turned my trike 90 degrees, saving me from a nasty collision with a deep ditch.

When I was about 12 years old, I had an unusual experience. I dug out my mother's family Bible to look up some information. I opened it up somewhere in Isaiah (wish now I knew exactly where) and began to read. The words literally started to swim off the page and it freaked me out at the time. I believe God was trying to give me an important message but perhaps I wasn't ready to listen yet.

Since then, I have had very vivid, spiritual dreams that defy earthly explanation. There are no human descriptions to do justice to the amazing colours that I experienced in these dreams.

There was another dramatic encounter with a man that I now believe was an angel. I was working in North Bay at the time, around 1987, six years before my salvation, when a man came into the office and asked me one question: "Do you have a place in heaven?" Afterwards, he proceeded to go through the entire office and asked everyone else the same question. Then he left without saying another word. I remember not sleeping very well that night and wrestling with God over this question, although I didn't realize at the time that that's what I was doing. This was a very important seed planted into me, although the fruit of it wouldn't manifest until six years later.

At the age of 32, I experienced the greatest miracle of all—salvation—and the number of miracles it took to get me to that place, I will never know! The Holy Spirit used the Al-Anon program to change my concept of who God is and, if it weren't for that miracle, I never would have come to God.

Another "God-incident" was finding a copy of the New Testament and Psalms in the yard of a house that we would later buy. This was miraculous because I found the book in August, when we first looked at the house. I went into the house and laid it on the mantle of the fireplace and, after taking possession of the house four months later, it was still lying on the mantle, exactly where I had left it! Nothing else from the previous owners was left in the house except that Bible!

Also, our neighbours who lived behind us had a stained glass cross in their door. One day, when I was doing dishes, I looked up and the sunlight was just at the right angle that the light was shining through the cross, directly at me. This was just prior to my conversion and I'm sure that it was another sign of how God was pursuing me.

After doing everything I could to cope with post-traumatic stress disorder, triggered by my mother's death in 1992, I finally realized that God was my answer. I was led to go to a healing crusade where I saw signs, miracles, and wonders right before my eyes! This was a huge miracle because I was raised

Catholic and I don't know what I was doing in this type of Pentecostal service. I was subsequently saved three days into the crusade. During this crusade, I received prayer for repeated bladder infections and I've not had one since!

The following are conditions that doctors, psychiatrists, and counsellors have spoken over me for a long period of time:

- post-traumatic stress disorder;
- depression/anxiety/panic attacks, including agoraphobia (fear of being out in public or in large, open places, which crippled me for years and almost kept me housebound);
- obsessive-compulsive disorder;
- fibromyalgia;
- arthritis;
- plantar fasciitis;
- irritable bowel syndrome;
- ovarian, breast, and anal cysts.

I suffered for over 20 years with these conditions. I've been on more medication than I can remember and was told I would be in a wheelchair long before now. In addition, I was practically bedridden with severe neck and back pain for two years, practically off my feet for another seven years, and told I would be on anti-depressants and anti-anxiety medication for the rest of my life. Although the last 20-some years have included a lot of suffering and torment from the demons responsible for mental illness, through it all, the Holy Spirit NEVER allowed me to accept that these were MY problems. He always told me, "This isn't you!" But it took years and years of prayer to build my faith to the degree where I've now overcome most of these issues, with full healing to be manifesting soon. Currently, I'm not on any medications, and I praise God for that!

Another thing that I had to learn to do during my many illnesses was releasing and renouncing doctors as idols or governing authorities over my life and health. But please don't get me wrong; I am not anti-doctor by any means! It's just that I used to place more value and authority over what they had to say, rather than what God said. Once I changed that and asked for God's wisdom as to what I was supposed to do with His temple—my body—He began to download information on changing my eating habits, incorporating alternative healing techniques (no, NOT new age), and other strategies, like detoxing. All these methods began to pay big dividends as my health improved slowly, but dramatically. I had to face a considerable amount of judgment by many well-meaning people as to what I was doing, since it was fairly "out there", but I knew I was being led by God. And His ways aren't man's ways, so I was confident on how I was being led. I also relied on the guidance of the Holy Spirit to know when and how to get off all the medications I was on. The Holy Spirit led me to a Christian chiropractor (whom I ended up leading to the Lord), as well as to a very gifted physiotherapist. Both of them continue to provide excellent therapy to me.

These are just some of the hundreds of miracles I've experienced, and I look forward to hundreds more!

Jenny Walton, Alliston, Ontario

When Jesus is All You've Got, He's All You Need!

Have you ever had a week or two with no rain? What about a month? Or even a year? It would really depend on where you live as to how long a drought may last. No drought is pleasant, but the worst droughts of all are the ones that personally affect us.

I remember years ago, while living in Barrie, Ontario, during a heat wave, when it hadn't rained for nearly a month, and the lush, thick grass was turning yellow and becoming very stiff and brittle. The creek near my home that once carried the sound of rushing water was now quiet and still; it had almost dried up completely. To make matters worse, the city officials had issued a strict water ban. People were not allowed to water their lawns or wash their cars in order to conserve water.

At first it wasn't so bad because things were lush enough that the absence of rain didn't seem to affect the gardens and grass, but soon that all changed and the gardens that were so full of life desperately struggled to survive.

Each night the promise of rain was heard in the distance as the thunder rolled and the wind picked up. The dark sky would turn bright as lightning shot across it. Surely rain was to follow, but over and over it seemed to skip past our house. Night after night you could hear the thunder and see the lightning, but still no rain came. One afternoon, dark clouds appeared and it looked like this was the downpour we had all been hoping for. Then it happened! We could see the pavement starting to become spotted with rain drops, but as quickly as the rain had started, it stopped again. It wasn't even enough rain to clear off the dust on the car windshield. The sun came back out and the heat continued with no relief in sight. Those who had air conditioning and extra water could manage a little better than those of us who didn't.

Needless to say, it did rain eventually, and the grass went from yellow to green and the flowers sprang back to life. But it left quite the impression on me as a youngster as to what can happen when you find yourself in the middle of a very dry season in life and you are without the resources to at least make it a bit more comfortable while you're going through it. Even though it took weeks for things to dry up, it only took days for things to spring back to life. You may be in a drought right now, but when God provides the rain, get ready to enjoy the harvest.

The following is our story as it relates to one of the driest seasons in my life. I hope and pray that you will see that my journey was not without perseverance, prayer, tears, and the amazing support of the Holy Spirit to guide us through.

Psalm 30, verse 5 says, "Weeping may last through the night, but joy comes with the morning." I made the analogy above because it describes the severe famine that took place in my life about 5 years ago. My wife and I often thought the abundance of rain was about to fall in our area of need, and at times it really did look like it would happen, but it always seemed to pass by, leaving us discouraged yet again and waiting for the next glimmer of hope.

At the time, my wife and I, along with our two small children, were facing one of the worst moments in our married life. We were a couple of weeks away from losing our house. We were told that in a few more days people would come to put a lock on our door and we would no longer have access to our home. It was being taken from us because we were so far behind on our mortgage payments. In total, we were about $12,000 behind and with no relief in sight. Oh yes, we had some sun showers here and there, and we were quick to thank the Lord for them. But it was never enough to impact our greatest need at the time, which was to get caught up on our mortgage. We had a small home, and we were a one vehicle family, so there was no luxury spending going on. It's true that to some a house is only bricks and mortar but it was the principle of the matter. It's one thing to sell your home, but it is a completely different matter when it gets taken from you.

We noticed, at this time, that many of our friends were beginning to judge us, as people often do when they find you in the middle of your process or trial, since that is often when you look your worst. We were given all kinds of advice from well-meaning individuals but these people were not in our position. Sometimes, when you're going through a struggle, it's easier for people to judge you than to help you. No one really knew that my wife had been sick and off work due to complications during the birth of one of our children, nor that I had about four jobs on the go.

It seemed so many people wanted to tell us how to cut back and not go out for dinner, or not get our hair cut as often etc., but they had no idea that we lived that way already. For us, to cut back was normal, not unusual. From the very beginning, I felt deep inside that we would come through, but that I would have to walk with Jesus step by step to make it. This situation was bigger than us, but not bigger than Him, and He was going to make a way where there seemed to be no way. That's easy to say now, but at the time, it seemed like just another promise that was meant for everyone else but us. Satan is a liar and a good one at that. He always tries to get us to disqualify ourselves from thinking that God would even consider doing a miracle for us.

One thing I knew was that I didn't have to allow the way I felt to determine what I did. At one of my lowest points ever, I made a decision and said, "God, I don't want to lose this home, but if I need to in order to get to where you are taking us as a family, then I will go through this with a good attitude." You see, I grew up on welfare because my mom chose to raise four children pretty much on her own, so we needed the financial aid. She raised us so that we had a great understanding that God answers prayer, and I witnessed miracle after miracle when I was growing up. My mom would pray and often the next day the answers would come. We didn't have much but, as children, we were abundantly loved by our mother.

I drew from that experience and began to tell God why I didn't want to lose the home, and how much it meant to my wife and children, and that I needed a miracle. I will never forget the day I came home from work, worn out from worry. I looked out to the back yard and my daughter, Hannah, who was six at the time, was twirling around, oblivious to the fact that, in a few weeks, she wouldn't have a backyard to play in. I looked at her and she made eye contact with me. Then she ran in the house, wrapped her arms around me and said, "Daddy, Jesus says it's going to be alright."

I started to cry because she had no idea what I was even thinking. But Jesus knew that I would listen to my daughter and so he used her to deliver that message just in the nick of time. My little daughter didn't even know that my heart was heavy at that moment.

During this time, my wife and I tried many times to pay something towards the mortgage, but the bank wouldn't accept anything unless it was the full amount. I remember thinking they were being nice to us by giving us an extension to come up with some money, only to find out that with that extension of time came a late fee of $200, as well as other fines, service charges, etc. Wow! I thought, if that was their kindness, I would hate to see them angry.

I even went in to see the bank manager to explain my situation, but her reply was very cold. I was told, "Sir, everyone has a story that they want us to believe." This crushed my spirit even further. To think that when you're already down, there are people who will push you down even further. I left her office and prayed, "Lord, forgive her because she doesn't understand." I left with my head down and, once again, felt ashamed, defeated, and embarrassed that I was in this situation in the first place.

I just wanted to quit. I was blaming myself that, as the husband and the head of my home, I couldn't provide well for my family. All I wanted to do was sleep or watch movies to find an escape from the worry and fear. I praise God for my wife, Donna, who never once made me feel inadequate along the way. If she ever felt frightened, she sure didn't show it. This was about an eight-month journey, but it felt like five years. We had no credit cards to draw from, no lines of credit, no wealthy family members to borrow from, no RRSPs to cash in, and no resources of any kind, so it was going to have to be God that brought us through. We had no plan B.

It's important to share that, during this entire process, my wife and I refused to stop giving to people, even if it meant giving very little. We didn't know how we were going to come through this difficult time, but we knew we would come through, leaning on each other, and strengthened by our relationship with Jesus Christ. We couldn't give money, so we would give clothing, etc. We were so determined not to allow this situation to steel our joy. Happiness is based on what happens, but joy is based on the strength of God for it's the joy of the Lord that gives us strength.

I desperately want people to know that I was no faith giant. One day I was up and the next day I was down. I would be strong one moment and weak the next. I felt like I had no business being in such fear and worry, yet I found myself there many times. But I must also say that I was quick to repent and did not allow myself to stay down for very long. Someone once said, "Kevin, you can't stop a bird from flying over your head but you can stop it from making a nest on your head." WOW! What an awesome thought. I can't stop all that is going on around me but I don't have to let it settle on me.

I know it to be true that a trial can bring us closer to Jesus than anything else ever could. But it can also drive a wedge in our relationship with Him. It's not that God loves us any less or walks away during a trial, but we sometimes believe that, if He loved us, this wouldn't be happening, so therefore He must not care. Such lies are of the devil, and I spent a lot of time casting those thoughts down and replacing them with the truth found in the Bible—that He is for me not against me, and that He is a very present help in times of trouble.

I finally got to the point where I realized something amazing. If I lost my home, I would still have what matters most—my wife and children. I realized that I was looking at what I was about to lose rather than what I was going to be able to keep. That simple thought brought much freedom to me.

My daughter remembers the day when I came home after work, looking rather sad, and said, "Hannah, let's go deliver some food to some people in need." We looked at what we had in the fridge, freezer, and our cupboards, and shared the little we had. We put together a box of food and drove to the home of a friend who was in need. We dropped the box off on their door step and ran away. It was great fun. I made sure that what I gave were good things that I would want to receive. I said to Hannah, "I want you to remember this day because you are going to see a turnaround in our situation, for God's Word says that whoever is generous to the poor lends to the Lord and He will repay him for his deeds."

The Miracle of Provision

Just about near the end of this journey, and with the lawyers closing in like a hawk about to grab a field mouse with no place to hide, I went upstairs in a desperate state. I was at my all-time lowest point. I put the shower on and sat down in the bathtub. (I know it sounds odd, but it's very relaxing.) As I was lying there, I felt nothing but the water hitting me like rain drops. In fact, I was pretty numb. I just didn't see any way possible out of this mortgage situation and we had nowhere else to move to. I am a fighter and a survivor by nature. I was a very good sales person, but what do you do when what you know to do isn't working anymore. I couldn't talk my way out of this, walk my way out, buy my way out, or even fight my way out. I WAS DONE!!!

I lay there and said, "God, I know you draw close to those who draw close to you, but I don't even have the strength to get up and come to you. I just feel so hopeless and like a failure to my family." Then, as I lay there, out of nowhere, an old hymn arose in my heart. The lyrics were: *"Love lifted me, love lifted me. When nothing else could help, love lifted me."* It was the Holy Spirit lifting me up!

I started singing it very quietly and with little strength, but then I got louder and sat up. Then I got louder still and stood up, and before I knew it, I was singing like an opera singer, "Love lifted me, love lifted me. When nothing else could help, love lifted me." I couldn't stop. It was wonderful. I felt so free all of a sudden that I didn't care anymore at all about the house. I just wanted to sing praises to God.

I got dressed and said, "Lord forgive me for all my waywardness. Here I am and I'm not giving up!" I went for a walk and started to pray and seek the Lord. I prayed for everyone else but me that day. I was so free! I just wanted to get my focus off of myself and onto others. It was liberating because, at certain points during this trial, I was starting to feel like I was in a box and all the sides of the box were mirrors reflecting my face and my agony back to me. It was nice to break free and realize that others were also facing difficulties and needed prayer—not just me. I think this was a key element in my maturing as a Christian. It helped me to be able to pull away from my own issues and begin to pray more fervently for others.

The following week, I made a decision to go to the mall to get some moving boxes, etc. I decided that if the answer I needed wasn't going to come, then I would at least get packing and do something to keep my mind occupied. And if the answer did come, then at least I would have an organized house.

I walked up to a store that sold moving supplies but the store was closed. I felt dazed since I was still a bit overwhelmed from all the months of pressure to get caught up on our mortgage. I peered into the office window and saw a sign above a desk that read, *"With God all things are possible."* I just stared at it. It might as well have been God writing on the wall since the message was so timely.

I decided to wait around since I wanted to find out if this person actually believed what it said on the sign, or if it was their way to get more business from "religious" type people. I was being a bit ornery, to be honest; yet deep inside, I was hoping this was a God-ordained appointment—and it sure was. After about an hour, a nice, tall man from Nigeria, now living in Canada, named Olaseni Soetan (Ola for short), walked past. This was his store. As soon as he spoke to me, I could tell he was indeed a very godly, young man.

For the next several minutes, he just spoke the words of the Bible to me, laid hands on me, and prayed. Then he did something very special. He said, "Kevin, how much money do you need?" He reached into his pocket, pulled out some money, and said, "Here my brother; you take this." I choked up and said, "Ola, thank you, but I just realized something; you giving me this money isn't what I came here for. God directed me here to get godly wisdom from you—not money. I shook his hand and left, but I left a changed man. I didn't even buy the moving boxes because I knew right then that I wasn't going to need them.

A few days after Ola had prayed that powerful prayer, things began to turn around. I met a person whom I hardly knew. He was feeling very down and needed encouragement. He sure didn't look like he had much himself and I felt bad for him. I felt the Lord asking me to encourage this individual. I chuckled a bit and thought, *"Lord you are funny that you want me to encourage this person when I still need encouragement myself."*

Nevertheless, for the next several weeks I encouraged him and never once mentioned my own situation. I just listened, and listened, and listened. Then one day, he said, "Kevin, you never talk about yourself; so tell me what is going on with you?" I felt it was okay to tell him because, up until this point, my wife and I had told very few people what we were going through.

I told this individual everything. It was like somebody had turned on a tap and everything that was stored up in me flowed out. When I was finished speaking, he couldn't believe all that I was facing and yet I was encouraging him. Then he said, "Well thanks for sharing. I will pray for you."

To be honest, when he said that, I kind of felt like saying, *"Oh great; what good will that do?"* because I had been praying a lot and seeing very little results. I know prayer is powerful, but I guess I was just getting so worn down in the process. I've learned that worrying is the biggest waste of time.

It does absolutely nothing to change the situation. During certain times of this trial, I found myself worrying more and more as my options to get out of this problem became less and less, and time was running out fast.

I just couldn't see a way out. Worry brought on fear, and fear was trying to lead me to hopelessness and then to depression. I had very little motivation to carry on with day to day tasks since I was consumed with this issue. It became all I could think about and the worst case scenarios would replay over and over in my mind. To combat this, I had to declare God's words over my life and situation more and more. One of the Bible verses that brought me the most comfort and that I clung to was Psalm 40, verse 2: "He lifted me out of the pit of despair, out of the mud and the mire. He set my feet on solid ground and steadied me as I walked along."

I felt this was my key verse that I needed to stand on because it wasn't a verse that just talked about where I was at now, but rather where God was going to take me. It was like the verse popped off the page, and it reignited my hope that better days were just about here. I could see myself being out of this situation and then sharing my testimony with others. This is exactly what I have been doing recently, and I've had the privilege to share this story live on a television program called "100 Huntley Street" in June of 2013. The title of the show was "Finding Pure Joy in Difficult Circumstances." I couldn't have said it any better. The fact that my wife and children were able to be on the show with me was all the more a testimony to God's goodness.

But back to the rest of the story! The following week, I went to see this new friend again. By now we were only a couple of days away from losing our home and I was still working very hard to provide the best I could. But it wasn't enough. I met with him one last time and, before we could say too much to each other, he reached in his pocket and said, "Kevin, I prayed about your situation." Then he slid a cheque across the table at Tim Hortons, where we had been meeting. I saw that it was made out to my name for $5,000. I was very grateful but, believe it or not, I handed it back and said, "Thank you, but I know your intentions are for me to use this towards the mortgage. However, the bank won't accept this because they want all or nothing. I didn't want to hand it back, but I felt it was the right thing to do. What he said next amazed me: "Kevin, that was the amount the Lord put on my heart to do, but then there is also the amount I personally want to do." Then he slid another cheque over the table for $7,000—for a combined total of $12,000!

What do you do when you've been in a process but then it suddenly ends? I will tell you what I did. I was in shock. I just stared at the cheques and then became a bit emotional. You see, it wasn't just about losing the house, but rather feeling like I had failed as the provider for my family. I had also begun to wonder if I had missed God on this. I thought that maybe I wasn't in faith, but rather in denial, and needed to just give up. Yet, for some reason, I just felt deep within that somehow I was going to come out of this victoriously if I kept obeying the voice of the Lord, and if I did not give up the fight of faith.

With these words, my new friend confirmed that this was a God-sized miracle. He said, "You will know that this is God because I don't want any of this money back. It is a gift. If you see me around, don't walk up to me and thank me or anything.

Just receive this from God." Then he said something that only God could have revealed to him: "God wants me to tell you that He has seen every act of generosity and every seed you have sown, even during your time of famine, and yes, He *does* hear you when you pray!" This person had no idea that my family had been doing this because I hadn't told him anything about that.

My wife was my biggest natural source of strength through this entire ordeal. When I came home, I dropped the cheques in her lap. She just started to cry. She muttered, "Praise God!" and wept again. Most husbands would have to agree that, when you have a great wife who has the right to find fault with you, but chooses instead to look at the potential in you, then she is not just a woman you are married to, but rather a gift that God has given you.

That afternoon, I took the children swimming and the water seemed cleaner than ever, the air seemed fresher than before, and the sun seemed brighter than I had ever remembered it to be. It was an odd experience, but all I could think of was that the burden I had been bearing must have been robbing me not only of strength but of my ability to enjoy the simplest things in life.

My wife then had a great idea, suggesting that I shouldn't just mail that cheque off to the bank but rather drive down to deliver it personally. So off I drove to Toronto to search out the collections department. I had no way of finding the lawyer that I had been dealing with on the phone, but while I was in the building, a door opened and before it could shut, I walked through it and made my way down the hall into a small office. While there, I heard a voice talking on the phone and I recognized it to be the lady who was assigned to my case. I called out her name and she came around the corner. I greeted her and gave her my first and last name. She knew then who I was and asked how she could help me. I asked her, "Do you remember when I told you that God was going to make a way for us to get caught up?... Well, He did!" I then gave her the cheque for the amount owing as well as a tract about the saving grace of Jesus Christ. She started to cry a bit and thanked me for being so kind to her.

In the end, all I can say is this: Praise God that, through this process, and even while sometimes doubting the Lord and His Word, His mercy and grace kept me from giving up altogether. There is an old song that goes like this: "If it had not been for the Lord on my side, tell me where would I be, oh where would I be?"

Praise God that He *is* on our side and I thank the Lord for my family and friends who stood with us in prayer during this time.

If I could leave you with any wisdom that I've discovered, it would be this: Don't stop finding ways to be generous, even when you don't feel like it. And don't try to figure out how, or when, God will do the miracle that you need. Just keep expecting, anticipating and trusting that He will. You can't be good enough to earn a miracle and you can't manipulate God to get one. But you can speak and read the Word of God over your life so that your faith can increase for what God will do for you in your own hour of need.

You never know who God will use, and is using right now in your life, to bring about a God-sized miracle just for you. He is no respecter of persons, the Bible says, and He is the same yesterday, today and forever. So if He did this for us back then, He can do it for you today! Even while you sleep, God is moving what you can't. So when you wake up, give Him praise and glory for what He has done through the night hours.

I pray this testimony has encouraged you. It is only one of the many wonderful things God has done over the years for my family. As a preacher, I now share this testimony with others wherever I speak or preach. No one can tell me that miracles are a thing of the past when I know for a fact that God did a miracle for me and my family, and is doing them every day for people all over the world. He is, and always will be, the one and ONLY miracle working God!

Kevin Rogler, Barrie, Ontario

He Healed Her! - Sarah's Story

In July of 2010, we had dear friends visiting from the US. Our older daughter, Sarah, who was 12 years old at the time, had been feeling discomfort in her upper abdomen for about a week. The pain wasn't consistent though and it seemed like it could be indigestion. Our family doctor was finishing up his holidays; so we decided to wait until he was back to decide whether or not to take her in, if the discomfort continued. The father of the family of friends who were staying with us is a doctor. One morning, during their visit, he and I were up earlier than others and I was asking him about some of Sarah's symptoms—including a new one which I had just become aware of that morning. He said that we needed to call our family doctor (who was just back from vacation that day), and request that she be seen as soon as possible. I did call, and our adventure began.

Our family doctor immediately called a pediatrician who met us at Royal Victoria Hospital, our local hospital here in Barrie. An ultrasound and MRI were quickly done and we were told that Sarah had a huge cyst that was beginning to block her common bile duct, causing her yellowing eyes and other symptoms. We later learned that Sarah actually had a rare disease called Choledochal Cyst Disease. It wasn't likely to be malignant, but we were told that it did need to be surgically removed, and whether or not that would be the end of it depended on the type of cyst and how much it may or may not have affected her liver.

The Sunday before Sarah's surgery, Sarah wasn't feeling well, so she and I stayed home from church—which, for us, is Connexus Community Church. The week before, the message had been from Romans 8. It stated how, in this world, there can be suffering—we, like all creation, groan as we wait for the wonderful future that the Lord has promised those who put their trust in Him. We were reminded that troubles in this world do not mean that God isn't with us or doesn't love us—it's just part of life in this sin-flawed world. We were reminded that no matter what, God will be with us. So Sarah and I went over those verses with no idea of how relevant and comforting they would become in the coming months.

We were told Sarah would likely be in the hospital for less than a week after the surgery. On August 5, we went down to Sick Kids Hospital in Toronto. The surgery went long, but well, and they removed the cyst, as well as her gallbladder and her common bile duct, both of which had been ruined by the cyst. They used a piece of her intestine to make a new common bile duct for her. The cyst had also attached itself to her liver, so they had to scrape one side of her liver. When she came out of surgery, she had a little bag coming out of her abdomen to drain any excess blood.

Sarah was recovering quite well for a few days, but then she developed blood in the drainage bag and her hemoglobin was dropping. They realized that she had an internal hemorrhage. They gave her a transfusion and things seemed to get better again. She was discharged home on August 15 but was having low fevers daily, which increased a little each day.

We had been told to call the hospital if she had a fever of 38.5° C or above. It hadn't reached that, but our friend from the US called and, being a doctor, he asked about Sarah's condition. I mentioned the increasing fever and he asked some very specific questions. Then he said that he believed Sarah had an abscess and asked me to take her back to Sick Kids Hospital immediately. He was very emphatic and so off we went to Sick Kids. Sure enough, she did have a serious infection and they admitted her right away. Imaging showed she had two bile leaks creating two pools of bile inside her abdomen.

On August 20, she was back in surgery again as they sought to find and stop the source of the leaks. Sarah came out of surgery still having the little blood drain bag, and now also a tube as well as a bigger bag collecting bile that was draining from her abdomen. The bile continued to drain, indicating that the leak wasn't stopping. So, on August 26, Sarah had an HIDA scan and MRCP which confirmed a continuing bile leak near her liver. On August 27, she underwent a third surgical procedure with the intention of putting in a stent to help the area drain and heal. It was supposed to be a quick procedure, taking an hour or an hour and a half. Four and a half hours later, the doctor came out and told us that he had tried repeatedly, and had even called in another doctor to help, but still could not place the stent.

The doctor who did the procedure said there seemed to be "no direct connection" between the duct that was leaking bile and the bowel that it was supposed to be connected to. This was very bad news. Sarah awoke after the surgery, vomiting and in pain. Instead of having a stent in place, she now had another bile drain and bag coming out between her ribs. I remember my husband, Bob, saying he felt sick.

We were told that, if indeed the duct wasn't connected, it would be a very difficult problem to correct. The duct was extremely small and the area that it needed to be connected to was inflamed from all the trauma and the constant presence of bile. The surgeon who had done her original surgery said that we should wait six weeks to see if the inflammation would go down some and then try again. It was beginning to look like Sarah could have a non-healing hole, leaving her not only with assorted tubes and bags draining her abdomen, but also leaving her at risk of major infection setting in.

On September 3, she had more symptoms and was readmitted for another 17-day stay at Sick Kids.

Throughout all this time, our family, and so many others, had been praying for Sarah. A special friend from Connexus, who has witnessed many healings, came to our home and prayed for Sarah's healing. The surgeries were all prayed for too. And yet, each time things seemed to go wrong and matters got worse instead of better. Each surgery was followed by days of pain, aggravated by Morphine which seemed to have a side effect of making Sarah unable to sleep. She would toss and turn, moaning and breaking our hearts.

These were difficult times indeed, but even so, we sensed God's presence and calming influence. Sarah did recover each time—quite quickly—and seemed to forget what she had just been through. She even "enjoyed" being in the hospital because of the kindness of the nurses and "Marnie's Lounge" which is a place for kids in the hospital to go to do all kinds of activities with other kids and staff.

The hospital provided her with a computer and all the movies she could watch. Either Bob or I stayed with her each night, sleeping in her room on a bed specially provided for parents. Bob works from home and my work had flexible hours, and somehow we both managed to do our jobs while staying at, and travelling back and forth to, Sick Kids each day. That in itself was an amazing blessing.

Our younger daughter, Rachel, who was 9 at the time, had her life turned upside down as well. But God also provided for her during that time. Our friends from the US were a great support, extending their stay when Sarah first got ill, and then coming back to stay with Rachel during a subsequent surgery. They prayed and talked with us regularly, always full of encouragement and wanting to hear all the details because of their love and concern. Also, a family that we had been acquainted with before played a huge role in helping us and Rachel through this difficult time. Their kids often kept Rachel company and gave her many reasons to smile. They were a God-send and were even happy to look after our puppy that we had just brought home two weeks before Sarah became ill. Through that time, our families became special friends and that is a continuing blessing. Our small group from Connexus was also very supportive, as were many other friends and family members. Through it all, God gave us comfort and strength. He provided for our needs, including Rachel's and our puppy Caili's. He helped us all to have a peace that kept coming back, despite times of turmoil and disappointment.

As the time was approaching for Sarah's fourth surgery, in mid-October, the surgeon ordered some scans in order to have a good sense of where everything was before going in. This surgery was to attempt to reconnect the tiny duct that wasn't connected and was leaking bile into her abdomen. To his shock and delight, the tests showed that the duct was, in fact, connected to her bowel and the leak was healing!!! You can imagine how thankful and overjoyed we were. The surgery was cancelled and, a couple of months later, on January 7, 2011, Sarah had her last surgery. This one was not to attempt to fix the leak, but only to take out the remaining drains because the leaks and duct were all healed up!

The surgeon didn't see this as a miracle. He thought a mistake had been made and that the duct had been connected all along, despite the other doctor's conclusion that is wasn't connected, and despite the constant leak of bile.

Personally, I suspect that it truly was disconnected and God connected it for us. In any case, He healed her! When things seemed the darkest, God just made it light—and I am so thankful to Him for it. Sarah came through everything still smiling. Through it all, she kept a positive attitude and was an amazing trooper as she lived for almost six months with a lot of uncertainty, discomfort, sometimes real pain, and always tubes and bags hanging out of her from every angle. She was even in a Christmas play with her bags taped to her back, under her angel costume. I never heard her question God or wonder why it was happening to her. I did remind her of the passage from Romans 8, and we did discuss the ways that we sensed God's help and presence, despite the ongoing problems. She seemed at peace with all that happened and still seems to look back, almost fondly, on the whole experience. She decided, during the time in hospital, that she'd like to become a nurse.

So that is Sarah's story. I look back at it with great thankfulness. It's a reminder to me not to fear uncertainty because, as we trust Him, we can be certain that God will never leave or forsake us—He'll be with us through all that life may bring our way. He has all power and still today heals bodies and hearts. I know some stories end differently—some children die—and it's so difficult to understand and accept these things. God is able and does heal. We are called to trust Him either way though. Whether healing comes in this life or the next, we will all experience complete healing as we trust Him for it, and we can rest assured that we can always count on His presence to see us through whatever comes.

Sue Black, Barrie, Ontario

Thy Faith Hath Made Thee Whole

I came to know the Lord in 1991, and what an exciting and amazing walk with Jesus I have had.

Back in 1978, before I was saved, I had a mole appear on my leg. A mole is described as a dark-coloured growth on the skin. My doctor called me in to tell me that I needed surgery to remove it. All went really well. Afterwards, my doctor told me that he had four people with this issue and I was the only one that came through it so well. We now give all praise to God. But it was not until 1991, when I received Jesus as my Lord, that I realized God's hand was on me even then.

Then, on April 5, 1993, after having a shower, I was led to look at my back and saw another light brown mark there. My husband, David, and I took this to God. I knew in my spirit what it was and thanked Jesus for bringing it to our attention. At a family gathering, they all prayed for me. David had his hand on my back and it was very HOT. In fact, it burned all the way home. Just before arriving home, in a very loud voice, I heard God say to me, "When you get home, read Mark 10:46-52." I had never heard the voice of God like that before. As soon as I got home, I read the verses where Jesus told blind Bartimaeus, "Go thy way; thy faith hath made thee whole."

How I hung onto that verse! In November and December, the mole really started to bother me and it was quite sore and painful. Oh, the faith that Jesus gave me! I never had

75

the thought—not even once—to go to the doctor. I knew, I knew, I knew that I was healed! And what was so amazing is that I never looked at that mole. Now that is God!

One day, in many of our prayers, it came up that someone I knew from the past had told me that he went to see a fortune teller and she told him that one day I would die from cancer. My husband, David, instantly broke that curse off my life. Thank you Jesus for showing us that! I believe it was the next day, while David was shaving and I was getting out of the shower, he told me to turn around. He was all excited and shouted, "That mole on your back is completely gone!" Talk about a miracle! How overjoyed we were. Praise God, Praise God!

What a day that was to witness the power of our God and how He loves us. I have shared this with many people and told them not to look at their circumstances. God is not a God of circumstance. If I had glanced at that mole, it could have negatively affected my faith. We just need to stand on the promises of our wonderful God.

Margaret Speare, Barrie, Ontario

Angel of Veterans Affairs

Recently, I was awakened at 2:00 a.m. and could not fall back to sleep. Our pastor's wife, Charlene, had mentioned sharing testimonies the previous Wednesday night, when I wasn't there, and early that morning, I felt compelled to share this one. Since I couldn't sleep, I began to write it down.

This is something that I have never, ever mentioned to anyone. Firstly because I don't think that anyone would believe me, and secondly because they would probably think that I just fell off the turnip truck.

Allow me to give you a little bit of background here. George, my husband, was born in Newfoundland and his mom gave him up when he was "old enough to touch the doorknob." When he was of age, he joined the army and spent 7 days in jail because there was no record of him anywhere and the men in power thought he was a spy. That makes me laugh because George was often challenged by the least little thing.

When we were married, I came across a little green book that had his military badge number in it and I asked him if he had ever seen his file. He replied that he had not and that he didn't want to talk about it. I remember smiling at the time because, knowing George, I can't imagine the tons of potatoes he had to peel during his stay with the army. He probably didn't want to remember those days.

The thought of his file just wouldn't leave me and, as the years went by, with prayer, I often would do some research in an attempt to locate it. I worked for the Ministry of Government Services and had access to certain resources. My mom and dad had always supported the Royal Canadian Legion and there was a man, named Mr. Vincent, who was renowned for locating files, pensions for widows, and benefits that the veterans didn't even know they had a right to. I knew this man and I eventually asked him if he could locate George's file, but to no avail. There was just no record of George Hann, Artillery Division, in our Canadian Army. He was in Korea; how could there not be a file?

Over the years, I had to admit George to four, yes four, nursing homes. That in itself is a story. Usually, when a patient is admitted to a nursing home, they come out in a pine box—not for a ride home. I don't know what the situation is now, but at that time, the Ontario Health Insurance Plan (OHIP) would only keep patients like George in a hospital for one month and the family would have to assume the costs, on a daily basis, after that period of time, until the patient could be moved to a nursing home. Those costs were absolutely ridiculous back then; I can't imagine what they are like now. The 9th floor of the Laurentian Hospital was designated as a nursing home and, as soon as space was available, George was transferred.

This "missing file" issue kept coming up but I just didn't have the time to look into it any further. Dr. Ali, a neurologist (one of Sudbury's finest), told me that George would never come out of his condition. His words were, "With the technology that we have today, your husband's brain is only this big." With his fingers, he made a circle about the size of a toonie.

I was quite overwhelmed. It had been a very difficult month—even worse than usual—if that was possible. There was just so much going on!

I had taken a few days off from work and, as I climbed into bed that night, I prayed the following prayer: "Father, I am just so tired. I don't have a clue what to do. I am so overwhelmed that I cannot see the forest for the trees. If there is something that you want me to do, or a direction that you want me to take, YOU are going to have to tell me loud and clear." I fell into a deep sleep and woke up feeling very, very strange.

For some reason, I walked up to my computer and noticed a telephone number there that I did not recognize. I remember picking up the paper, taking my glasses off, and holding it very close to my face. I still did not know what this number was and I asked myself, *"Is that my handwriting?"*

I also remember being very aware of how good I felt. I felt alive, maybe even happy. I started to do some chores and it is not unusual for me to put my own melody to words as I work. While I was singing, "All glory and honour be to God, all glory and honour be to God,...for what He is doing and will do, for what..." suddenly I heard a voice say, "Dial the number."

I was somewhat annoyed because I was actually having a good time, and I couldn't imagine the number being of any importance. However, I dialed the number and I knew—I just knew—that I was speaking to an **ANGEL**. I believe that there is power in our words and, as God is my witness, may he strike me dead right here, right now, if the following isn't exactly as it happened, with absolutely no exaggeration and no lies. I put my hand to my brow and managed to say, "My name is Claudette Hann. I am married to George Albert Hann. George was in the military. His badge number was, I think, 14263 and there is absolutely no file to be found. The ANGEL replied, "I know; I have the file and someone from North Bay will be in touch with you next week." Then the phone went dead.

On Wednesday of the next week, Kim, from North Bay's Veterans Affairs met me on the 9th floor and evaluated George's condition. I signed a few papers and Kim said that she would meet with me again on the following day, at the same time. The following day, Kim handed me a $13,000 cheque, the exact amount of money that I needed! I looked up at her and said that I did not have the money available to pay the taxes on this cheque. Kim informed me that there were no taxes to be paid. I asked, "Are you sure?" She laughed, gave me a hug and said, "I'm sure."

Veterans Affairs paid for each of the four nursing home stays, his hearing aids, glasses, and even a custom-built wheelchair, slightly tilted, so that when he was better, he could not just walk away. To this day, I still receive a $336 cheque monthly, tax free.

The following week, I tried the number again. I did not believe that I had a direct line to St. Peter's receptionist in heaven. This time, a woman answered, "House of Commons." Who calls the House of Commons? Do you know of anyone who has called the House of Commons?

I know that there are groups of prayer warriors who pray for only specific things. One of these groups prays for the leaders of our nation and the parliament, including the House of Commons. They pray for justice and restoration. I know that my prayers, one on one, to the Father are heard, but I sincerely believe, **with all of my heart**, that if it were not for this group of intercessors, I would not have had such a favourable outcome. I probably wouldn't have had any success whatsoever! After all, it had been years of searching with no results.

But for **HIS GRACE** and **MERCY** and for the **POWER OF PRAYER!**

Claudette Hann, Angus, Ontario

Signs and Wonders Healing Miracle

I am a walking miracle! I'd like to share a Scripture that will explain what I am talking about. It is from Psalm 107, verses 19 and 20: "Then they cried to the Lord in their trouble, and he saved them from their distress. He sent out his word and healed them; he rescued them from the grave." (NIV) I believe that's where I have been rescued from; that is the healing that I've received.

My journey actually started in 2010 when I was suffering headaches, but in January 2011, I was diagnosed with throat cancer. The throat cancer in itself was alarming. So I prayed and I prayed, and in my prayers, God answered me three times: "It's not your time." That put me at rest, but one of the big concerns came when I first saw the surgeon and he mentioned that it's cancerous and that I would require radiation and chemotherapy—possibly also surgery.

I saw the oncologist and he explained the situation more clearly. He told me that I had stage 4 cancer and that I only had a 40% chance of survival. Of course, I told the doctor that I don't have anything to worry about because God told me it's not my time yet; so everything will go well. Although God had told me that, I still worried. I know I should have trusted in God and in what He told me, but I still worried. So I prayed and I prayed again. Well, God got angry with me. He came to me in a dream. Normally I don't remember my dreams, but this one I clearly remember. I was at my own funeral, in my coffin, and suddenly I came out of the coffin. With an angry voice, God said, "Remember, I have the power of the resurrection; so trust Me when I say 'it's not your time.'" That put me at ease. I thanked God for that dream.

When the surgeon had told me about this cancer, he had set the dates for my treatments for radiation and chemotherapy. He wanted me to have the treatments while I had planned to be on a missions trip, but I told him, "No, God's work is first." He said it would increase my chances of survival. But I told him that God would take care of me. So I went on my missions trip as planned.

The Monday after I returned from my missions trip, I started my treatments at Princess Margaret Hospital. In June of 2011, after all the treatments were done, I had to go back to see the surgeon again. He checked me out and told me that he'll have to remove some lymph nodes in my neck because they were very swollen. It turned out that it was a good thing they removed them because they were very cancerous as well. But before the surgery took place, they had to tell me about some of the possible effects and the concerns. One of the concerns was that there was a 70% chance of cutting my neck nerve. I asked the surgeon what the implications of that were. He said, "Well, if I cut the nerve, you'll have restricted left arm movement, and if you reach above your head, it will be painful." I responded, "Ok, I'll pray and pray, and I will ask the Lord not to let the surgeon cut my nerve—I will ask that He would please guide the surgeon's hands so that he doesn't cut my neck nerve."

In July of 2011, I had my surgery. The first thing that I did when I woke up from the surgery was check my arm. There was no pain and no restrictions in my arm movement. So I thanked the Lord for guiding the surgeon and not allowing him to cut my nerve.

The next day, the doctor came in to check how I was doing. He walked in with his head bowed down and said, "I'm sorry, but I cut your nerve." But then I showed him my arm and said, "See, God healed me. I have no pain; no restrictions in my arm." His jaw dropped and he replied, "That's never happened before." So obviously, I got a miracle. GOD HEALED ME! Why? I don't know! Why does God heal? When He heals, and how He heals is a mystery. God doesn't explain why He does it. But I was very grateful for this healing.

In October of 2011, I had to go in to have my feeding tube replaced. I had to be tube-fed because I had trouble swallowing and chewing, and they had to replace the tube every six months. This is because there was no saliva production and the throat muscles had been cut. When I went in to see the doctor, I expected the usual procedure, which is a quick pulling out of the old feeding tube and putting in a new one. It usually takes only about five minutes. However, when the doctor started pulling, I had pain. He looked at me and said, "That's strange. I'll give it a bit of freezing." Then he pulled again and there was still pain. He said, "I better x-ray that." After the x-ray, the doctor asked if I had lost weight and I replied, "Yes, I lost 35 pounds. Why?" He told me that my stomach shrunk and half of the feeding tube had come out of my stomach. This could have been fatal because the food would have gone into my peritoneum. It's like having a ruptured appendix. So I told him, "Well, God plugged those holes to the feed. Only one hole was open and it went into my stomach, where it was supposed to go. That's my second miracle!"

God had said to me, "It's not your time," and He showed it to me through the miracles, the healings, and everything that He has done for me. I thanked the Lord, and said, "There's got to be a reason why you've done what you've done. Now what do I need to do?" He told me that He wants me to give my testimony to everyone I come across, believers and non-believers alike. For believers, it is to reaffirm their faith; but for the non-believers, it is to plant a seed of faith—or, if a seed has already been planted, to add the water to nourish it so that they will become a believer. And it's only because of the Lord, Jesus Christ, that I am able to do this.

A year ago, I was very weak. Because of the radiation treatment around my neck, there was a lot of burning and irritation and destruction inside my throat. But my healing took place, and I got better and better. I was having trouble speaking. I could not come to church until December because my feedings took about two hours each time, and I had to have six feedings a day with a rest of about two hours in between. It took all day just for the feedings! It was very difficult, but eventually I was finished with that. I was able to increase my activities and God gave me strength.

I have been able to give my testimony at my church and I've also been asked to speak at various other locations. I even made a video that will be shared with whoever wants to view it to see that God is there for us. That's what we have to remember. God is always there for us—for spiritual healing, physical healing, or mental healing—he's there for us. There are many stories in the Bible, in the Old Testament and the New

Testament, where healings occurred, and healings still occur today through God's touch. We have to remember to trust in Him at all times—even when it's hard. And it's through Jesus Christ that we're able to go on and move ahead. I thank Him for that!

Norman Tretter, Barrie, Ontario

Grandpa's Miracle

Each and every person has a showcase in the portals of their mind. Many of the trophies have stood the test of time and are reminders of the faithfulness of God.

Memory is one of the greatest gifts that God gives to us. Without it, we would live mundane lives without being able to cherish the pictures in our minds that bring a smile to our face and joy to our heart.

Hardship is a great teacher and much is learned from walking "through the valley of the shadow of death."

The story that I want to share is one that involves hardship and a walk through the valley I just mentioned. It is also a trophy in my showcase that brings a smile to my face and joy to my heart. This story took place in the early 1990s.

I was taking a Telecare training course in order to man the phones at the Telecare office. It was a service provided for those who just needed someone to talk to. We watched a documentary about a woman who had died of cancer and we had to talk about the effects of the death on the family. After that, we had to tell a personal story involving our own experiences with death.

The following is the story that I told:

We had a young lady, who had a two-year-old boy, living with us. She looked after our children after school in exchange for room and board. Just before Christmas, the little boy went with his father to Hamilton to visit his grandfather. I came home from the store that we owned very late that night and was extremely tired. The mother of the little boy called me and asked me if I could take her to Hamilton because her little boy was very sick. I told her that I could not possibly drive that far since I could hardly stay awake, but if she would call me after I had a couple of hours of sleep, I would take her. The next thing that I remember is my husband leaning over me, as he woke me up the next morning, saying, "One of us has to take Stacey to Hamilton. Timmy is dead." I felt as though someone had hit me over the head with a two by four. I could not believe it.

Stacy and I cried all the way to the grandfather's house. As soon as we entered, the grandfather said, "Anyone who has been in contact with Timmy may die. He had meningitis." My first thought was of my children. They could all die.

I remember my hands trembling as I dialed the phone to tell my husband to call the doctor and tell him what had happened. I did not know God well at the time and was told to seek medical help as soon as possible. All the way back from Hamilton, I thought about the possibility that all our children could die from this infectious disease. I came to a realization, after talking with God, that even if all my children died, I would still follow Him. I had made a decision to trust Him when I was nine years old and I knew that He was trustworthy, in spite of circumstances. Little did I know at the time that I would later be tested on that truth, when our 35-year-old son died suddenly of a heart attack.

While I was telling this story to my group, my husband came to the door. I knew something was wrong just by the look on his face. He told me that his father had a stroke and was in the hospital in Toronto. The people in the group prayed for me and for Jim's family before we left to go see Jim's father. I called my sister and asked her to get her friends to pray.

When we got to the hospital, grandpa was strapped to a gurney; his eyes were all filmed over and I thought that he would never be able to see again. He did not speak as he was in an unconscious state. I prayed silently over him as I laid my hands upon his head. I felt fire going through my hands but nothing visibly happened. I stayed for several hours and, the next day, I brought a disc player and let him listen to beautiful music while he was in the comatose state. I prayed while he listened. I had contacted everyone that I knew across Canada and asked them to pray. One pastor prayed with me over the phone every day. I had never known anyone who had been healed but just believed that it was the right thing to do. I needed to pray and ask for mercy from our Father in heaven to save grandpa. We loved him and did not want him to die.

I did not know much about the power of prayer but was desperate to see God work in my father-in-law's life, because I knew that Jim's mother would be lost without him. Jim's mother was very dependent on her husband, since she did not drive, and was quite a fearful person. She did not like to go out, and did not join in most family gatherings, because she would end up sick. Now I know that fear produces those results. Grandma could not even go to the hospital because she was so upset. I had just learned how important it is to replace worry with prayer, so I told her to just pray for grandpa every time she thought of him. I told her it was important for her to do that; otherwise she would become sick herself. I know that bit of knowledge helped her because she was considerably more calm than she normally would have been.

Grandpa was moved to a private room in preparation for his expected departure from this world. On Tuesday, the doctors called the family together and told us that the stroke that Mr. Darlington had was in the worst part of the brain and, if he recovered, he would be in a vegetative state. They wanted to know if we wanted him put on a ventilator if the need arose. We all agreed that we did not want grandpa to live on a machine. That would not be living.

I looked at the doctors and said, "I guess all we can do is pray." They rolled their eyes to the back of their head as if that were a really crazy idea.

On Wednesday, we took our children down to the hospital to see grandpa, but he did not respond in any way. We thought it might be the last time our children would see their grandfather alive. However, on Thursday morning, grandpa sat up in bed and started to talk. Everyone was amazed. He could even count by sevens backwards. No brain damage!!

The doctors called us back into the same room where they had given us the bad news and said, "This is a very humbling experience for us. Obviously, what we have here is a miracle." Everyone looked at me, and I looked to heaven and said, "Praise the Lord!"

Grandpa lived for eleven more years. He came to live with us for a short time and left us a house as our inheritance. I praise the Lord for this miracle and, whenever I hear about a situation that the doctors have called inoperable, incurable, or hopeless, I think of grandpa. "NOTHING is impossible with God."

Sue Darlington, Barrie, Ontario

From Surviving to Thriving

The morning began like any other, except for the fact that my two youngest children were slightly late getting out the door to catch the school bus. My oldest daughter, Kayla, had already left earlier on her high school bus. As on previous similar occasions, I decided to drive my two youngest, Alyssa and Kyle, to their school since I had to head out for a work staff meeting that morning anyway. I have very little memory of what happened after I dropped them off at school.

It was January 2008, in Oro-Medonte, Ontario. We usually have a lot of snow and ice at that time of year in our area. On the way out of the school, I hit a patch of black ice and lost control of the car. Although I have no recollection of the crash, a school bus heading in the opposite direction hit me head on. The children in the school yard, including my own kids, heard the bang, but they didn't know that I had been in that collision.

When I reflect back on what happened to me that day, I know that God was in this from the first second. There are just too many amazing details for me to consider them as coincidences.

I was told that my children's bus driver came on the scene instantly to lift the roof up off me, to allow me to breathe. A police officer friend also arrived and was sent to relay the news of the crash to my children and their principal. The principal,

Melody Northrop, instantly knew that it was me who had been in the accident. Both the principal and the family friend were members of our church and they immediately prayed for me at the accident scene before any medical help arrived.

I worked as an office administrator for our church and was on my way to work to attend a staff meeting with my boss, Pastor Carey Nieuwhof, and several other leaders of Connexus Community Church. At the time, we were working out of one of the elders' home. Pastor Carey had apparently left a message for me, saying that he was running a little late for the staff meeting because he was stuck in a traffic jam caused by an accident just ahead of him on the highway. Little did he know that I was in that accident!

When he passed the scene of the accident, he realized that the vehicle was mine and stopped to see what he could do to help. I believe that it was an act of God that He sent so many members of my church family to be by my side and pray for me right from the start. But this was only the beginning of a very long journey. Pastor Carey then went into the school to speak to and try to comfort my children. Kayla was writing a high school exam that morning and would be finished school very early. Carey waited for Kayla so the children could be told together.

The closest hospital to the scene of the accident was Royal Victoria Hospital, in Barrie, Ontario. However, I was later told that if I had been taken there by ground transport ambulance, I would not have survived. As I mentioned, the winter weather conditions were extremely bad that morning, and a call was placed to have a helicopter airlift me to Sunnybrook Hospital in Toronto. This decision was vital to my survival. The helicopter dispatcher, Melissa, also happened to be a member of our church. She dispatched the helicopter instantly, not realizing that it would be for someone she knows. I was the only helicopter admission to the hospital that day due to the extreme weather conditions. No other helicopters were allowed out. The fact that one was sent out for me also had to be an act of God.

I did not have a lot of support from family at this time of my life, but God brought people from my church family to be at the right place, doing the right things, at the right time.

At Sunnybrook Hospital, the emergency team kept me alive one hundred and twenty seconds at a time. My physical body gave up several times, but something kept me going. I believe it was prayer! God let me know that people were there for me. I was told that 80 or more people showed up in the waiting room at Sunnybrook Hospital and began to pray for me. They eventually had to be told to leave because the room was so overcrowded. I wonder if that had ever happened before.

I was in a coma for 16 days, I think. I believe that an unconscious person's spirit is alive and can hear, even when their mind cannot hear and their body cannot react. My children were told to say "goodbye" to me because I wasn't expected to live. The younger ones, Kyle and Alyssa, were 9 and 12 at the time, and I'm sure this news must have devastated them. Kayla was 15 years old, and I was told that she refused to give up on her mom. She stubbornly insisted that I would come out of this coma and that I would be fine. I believe that my spirit heard her child-like faith, strengthening my body to strive to live.

The kids were on their own at this point. Because of difficulties with my ex-husband, the children really had no family home to go to when I was admitted to the hospital. They had no dad at home and no relatives to take care of them. My police officer friend got children's aid involved to obtain care for the children. Once again, my church family stepped in. Two beautiful people, a couple from my Bible study, took my kids into their home! They made sure that they made it to school every day; made meals for them, and catered to them in a God-loving, caring way. I know that God was taking care of my children. Melody made sure they had lunches and were able to participate in school trips; teachers also helped with driving them home.

I spent months in the hospital and had many surgeries. My first surgery was on my face. The surgeons needed a photo of me to do the reconstruction because my face had been destroyed beyond recognition during the crash. I suffered three skull fractures, was unable to eat, and needed a tracheal tube to breathe. I also had double vision in one eye. The reconstruction of my face required 13 plates. My jaw was rebuilt and my eye was completely restored.

Then came the other surgeries. I had fractured 6 vertebrae in my spine. I had a crushed left shoulder and lost most of the deltoid muscle. It was removed because there was too much damage. The forearm was also crushed. It was strengthened with plates during one of the surgeries. Referring to my right elbow, one surgeon said that, "I left it on the road!" It was not there anymore. They operated on my right elbow but it became infected, and they had to operate on it a second time. The surgeons did the best they could but the arm would still just hang there like a rubber band. It would bend forwards and backwards with no joint in it.

Due to the six fractured vertebrae, I was put in a full body brace until May and couldn't move at all. It's a miracle that I didn't come a smidgeon closer to hitting and destroying the spinal cord because the surgeon said I would have died, or been paralyzed for life, had that been the case. My right leg suffered a tibia plateau fracture, which means that there was a split right down the middle. My knee and leg were wrecked! I had also broken my left ankle.

Many times there was a waiting room full of prayerful friends supporting me at the hospital. My mom did not believe in God, but the ordeal I was going through brought my mom back into my life. This too was an act of God, bringing some restoration back into my family.

When I first began to wake up from being in the coma, I started to remember things. I could feel people were praying for me. I could just sense it. I still went in and out of consciousness, and I remember feeling lost and defeated. My mind was telling me that I don't want to do this anymore. I didn't want to go on. I felt hopeless and wanted to give up. At one time, I felt like I was in a dungeon. Then I saw a huge, bright operating room. I sensed God telling me, "Cindy, you're going to be OK. I will make sure you will be alright. And your kids will be OK too!" This vision gave me the steady peace and the unbreakable strength to go on with whatever I had to face. I knew that God was with me. I was told that Greg Armstrong, our former youth minister, was with me at the time.

During the months of recovery, I had to learn to eat and walk again. Chewing and swallowing was very difficult due to the rebuilt jaw. I had to receive artificial saliva to help me eat and process food. Learning to walk was also challenging. The physiotherapists and nurses were very helpful and patient with me. On March 13, I was transferred from Sunnybrook Hospital to our local Soldiers' Memorial Hospital, in Orillia. My rehabilitation continued there and I slowly began to walk again.

Four months after the accident, on April 6, 2008, the nurses allowed me to have a birthday party in the Nurses' Room for my daughter, Alyssa. She was turning 13, and that day, I sat up in a wheelchair for two hours for the first time to celebrate with her. It was a great day for both of us.

When I was able to go home, I was excited, but still very limited in the things I could do for myself and my children. A friend from my Bible study group worked for a lawyer. Without his legal help, I would never have been able to deal with all the insurance issues and obtain the best care for my disability and rehabilitation. A team of seven professionals regularly cared for me in my home. I had a Personal Support Worker to help with personal hygiene and dressing, a Rehabilitation Support Worker to help with bills and organization, an Occupational Therapist to teach me to do work-related things on my own again, a Speech and Language Pathologist for brain training and speech improvement, a Physiotherapist for retraining my limbs to work again, a Nutritionist to help me with my diet so that the medication wouldn't continue to add unhealthy weight, and a Case Manager to ensure that everyone was working together for the best outcome in care for me. God again provided for all my needs.

During this time, many ladies from church helped provide for me and my children by bringing home-cooked meals to our home. Other friends provided transportation for me and my children. I still had to travel to Sunnybrook Hospital in Toronto three times a month for follow-up appointments with doctors. During one of these visits, Dr. Axlerod told me that he could not fix my "loose arm". He lightheartedly called it my "noodle arm" because it hung like a noodle without a joint. He referred me to a specialist, named Dr. King. Friends were always available and willing to drive me all the way to London, Ontario, for my appointments with him.

Dr. King was a grumpy specialist. "I'm going to make you smile someday," I said to him with strong faith. By this time, my attitude had become very positive. I had become one of the most grateful persons, and my smile usually showed it. The doctor discussed the options for my arm with me. There were three choices: 1) I could receive a partial joint replacement for my elbow, but this had never been done before, and the doctor expressed his fear to perform this surgery on a young person; 2) he could fuse the elbow and make it stiff, with no mobility; 3) he could amputate my arm.

I prayed for wisdom and I had peace with my decision. I wasn't worried. After all, God had told me that I will be OK! I was hoping for # 1 as it was the best scenario. The surgery was performed and it was such a great success that the doctors used my case to write a report in a medical journal to reveal the technique and to teach other surgeons the procedure. The results were awesome! I can use my arm for almost anything now, with full mobility, and I made Dr. King smile! As usual, God used this seemingly terrible situation and made something good out of it.

My full recovery took a long time—5½ years to be exact—but 26 surgeries later, I'm fully functional again. Although I still suffer with daily chronic pain, it's manageable. It sometimes slows me down, but it doesn't control me or prevent me from doing the things I want to, or have to do. I do some things differently, but I can do them! God also taught me that it's OK to ask for help. You have to be humble to do that, and it is His will that we be humble.

I believe that God is using me and my experience to glorify Him for the healing. He is the reason why I lived and why I am whole again. I am very thankful to Him for providing excellent medical care and I'm extremely positive in attitude and thinking, despite the challenges I've had. I want to tell others how wonderful God has been to me from the moment of my accident to this day. I am grateful because I've learned a lot and there is nothing I can't do! God took me and "cradled" me.

I've always enjoyed my working days and was grateful for my job as an office administrator at my church, but deep down inside, I had always wanted to be a "stay-at-home mom". Now I get to be a stay-at-home mom and can still provide for my children. That's all the work of God! He's been in on this journey with me from the first moment on. And I'd even take this healing journey all over again if I had to.

I'm stronger in my faith, I have immense love for people and I'm truly happy. You could say I'm a new person in body, mind and spirit...as if I were born again *again*! I'm no longer judgemental and I accept people for who they are. My ultimate wish is to help others and to encourage them too.

Note from the Editor, June 3, 2014: When I met with Cindy to record her story, I saw a woman with a beautiful smile, a beautiful face and a beautiful attitude. After all that her body, mind and spirit had been subjected to during and after her car accident, I was amazed to see her as beautiful as she was before—inside and out. As one of the church members who regularly prayed for Cindy's full recovery, I praise God for this healing miracle!

Cindy LaTour, Barrie, Ontario

Living by Faith

Living by faith was a principle that I had exercised from the very beginning of my walk in Christ. If I had come to Christ by faith, then I was determined that I would not go back to trying to figure things out in my brain. After all, if my brain had led me down wrong pathways for the first twenty years, it was not suddenly going to change its thinking patterns. I made a conscious resolution that I was going to live life from the heart and, as far as was possible, make my major decisions based upon what my heart was telling me to do. I just turned 75, and it has been pretty much like that for the last fifty-four years of my life.

When my wife, Pauline, and I immigrated to Canada from England, we left well-paid teaching jobs behind. Pauline stayed home to raise the kids and I preached in a small start-up church, in Painswick, where I received the princely sum of fifty dollars a week. We both supplemented this income by driving school bus. We prayed about every need and there were many of them. We didn't qualify for OHIP (Ontario Health Insurance Plan) because we had not been in the country long enough.

There was one occasion when a kettle of boiling water spilled over my son, Mark. His chest and arms were covered in red scald marks. Because we did not have money to pay for a doctor, my wife wrapped him in cold bandages and I prayed aloud to God. Mark went to sleep. When he awoke two hours later, the burns were gone. We both had witnessed a miraculous intervention by the Lord!

Numerous were the times when we proved God to be our great provider. One day, I went to the muffler shop to get my car exhaust fixed. There were several people waiting around. The mechanic was stretched on his back, examining a car. All that I could see were his feet sticking out. Suddenly he spoke and said, "The winner of the Lottario came from Barrie this week and won $100,000." I shouted back, "A hundred thousand dollars wouldn't pay for what I've got under the third button of my shirt." There was no reply, but a lady with iron grey hair came up to me and said, "What have you got under the third button of your shirt?" I replied, "Jesus Christ lives under there and He can live in you as well."

This lady then went on to tell me that she had had grand mal seizures, had severe heart palpitations, sky-high blood pressure, and tinnitus. I said, "Well, read James 5:14 and give me a phone call."

The next day, she called me and asked me if the elders of the church would come to her home and pray for her. She gave me the address as #1 Castle Drive. I didn't tell her that there were only two men in our church and that one of them was a new convert. He instantly became an elder and, that night, we went to the address she had given us. It turned out to be the castle that the road was named after—"Launt's Castle". This lady's name was Audrey Sarjeant, a member of the wealthy Sarjeant family in Barrie. We entered the house and, before long, Audrey received Christ as her Saviour. Then we anointed her with oil and prayed for her. We left and, within a week, she phoned with great joy to say that her CAT scans had come back clear, her blood pressure was normal, and she was feeling terrific. She never had a seizure again and became a member of our small and growing church.

Audrey had a cousin called Jean. Jean had recently been widowed. Audrey arranged for me to see this lady, who lived in Toronto. I prayed with her and she too received Christ. She returned to Toronto. Later that year, in the depth of the '76 winter, I found myself without money and without work. I refused to accept any unemployment benefits, believing that God and His angels would look after our family. One day, Pauline said, "We are out of food. What are we to do?" I replied, "Pray!" Then I went to the mail box, which was a mile away. I had just about enough gas to get me there. There was a single envelope in the box with a Miami post mark. When I opened it, there was a cheque for $2,418 and a note from Jean to thank me for helping her. She was giving me the fourth part of the residue of her husband's will.

Hallelujah! That was a lot better than an unemployment cheque for $80 from Pierre Trudeau!

There is a difference between being in the centre of your comfort zone as a Christian believer and living by faith on the brink of disaster. Our circumstances, during our years of preaching to the colonists in Canada, took Pauline and me very quickly from the safe seat in the boat to walking on water. God HAD to perform regular miracles or we were sunk.

On one occasion, in the depth of winter, I had a call from a man called Charlie Perrault. Charlie had a log house which he would fill regularly with young people for Christian retreats. It was a hundred miles due north in the boondocks. Charlie asked me if I would come up and preach for him. He had a house full of kids and had run out of sermons. It was six o'clock on a Sunday morning. Charlie said, "If you can find the gas money to get up here, we will get you home."

All I could rustle up was one dollar and some odd change. I put that into my gas tank, in a big 350 Chevy, and set off on a hundred mile trip with less than two gallons of petrol. This old car did about 15 miles to the gallon, so it was an act of insanity to think I could make it on Esso. The extra would HAVE to come from God. Thirty miles up the highway, the needle was on empty and I began to pray. One hand was in the air and the other on the wheel. Every time I brought my hand down, the engine began to cough. I drove 70 miles on fumes and faith before I pulled in to see my friend, Des Kerr. He had a jeep and drove us the next thirty miles, through the snow, to Charlie's cabin. After I preached, these kids gave me $80 to get home. I picked up my car at Des' house and asked for a can of gas to prime the engine because I knew the tank was as dry as the Gobi desert. When my friend began to pour the gas in the filler pipe, it overflowed immediately. The tank was full to the brim!

I proved two things from that episode. Firstly, that engines run better with NO gas at all; secondly, that God, who could feed five thousand people with five loaves and two fishes, finds no problem in filling the gas tank of a penniless preacher when He sends him to preach the true gospel of Jesus Christ.

One of my good friends, a man of great stature in the preaching world, was called Walter Best. His ministry had much impact in the town of Peterborough, where he pastored a large church.

One Monday morning, my phone rang. It was Elanor, his wife, asking me to join her at Princess Margaret Hospital, in

Toronto. Wally was in a coma after suffering a massive heart attack. He had been clinically dead for several minutes but, after skilled intervention, they had revived him. However, things were not good.

"No More Tears" baby shampoo was the only anointing oil I had in the house; so armed with a bottle of that, I set out for Toronto.

I was met by Elanor (a woman of strong faith), who directed me to the emergency facility. The beds, in this state-of-the-art ward, were arrayed in a circle like numbers on a clock face, with the nursing station in the centre.

Wally was lying at one o'clock on the dial. He was unclothed, with wires and tubes hanging off him. With permission from the nurse, I went to his bed, took his hand, and spoke his name. There was no reaction. It was time for the shampoo. I shook the bottle and about half the contents ended up on Wally's chest. When I prayed, I found my hands slipping among all the fixtures. I didn't think that God was worried about the lack of protocol. I just asked Him to rebuke death (which has a real presence), and to restore Wally to life and health.

Then I spoke in Wally's ear, "Remember, you are due to preach for me in November. Squeeze my hand if you are going to be there." Sure enough, still snoring in his coma, Wally squeezed my hand.

Later that year, Wally, the prince among preachers, preached from behind my pulpit—his first sermon after being discharged from the hospital—and it was a good one.

Faith in Christ and "No More Tears" baby shampoo had worked!

A Celebration of New Life

The voice on the telephone was tense and fraught with anxiety. "Pastor Wilson, come quickly, Joel is dying." It was Roxanne Smith, a young mother in my congregation, who lived with her husband, Mike, a few miles north, in Orillia.

"We are at the Soldiers' Memorial Hospital, waiting to be taken to Toronto," continued Roxanne, "but if you come now, you will be able to pray for Joel."

And "come" I did. On the way north, steering with one hand, I read a scripture from Luke 7, where Jesus gave John the Baptist His credentials: the deaf being healed, the blind receiving their sight and the dead being raised.

Fortified, I went to the emergency room where the six-month-old baby was lying in an incubator, as grey as paper, with an angry red lump above the forehead, where the Meningitis poison had gathered.

I asked the nurse to remove the lid and, with Mike holding my hand, I rebuked the power of death and commanded life and health for the child. Immediately the ambulance arrived but, before they whisked Joel away, I said to the parents, "Call me in twenty years time. I want to officiate at his wedding!"

The next morning, Joel was out of his coma, but a day later he was pronounced to be deaf because of brain damage. Roxanne recalled the scripture that I had given her, about the deaf being healed, and requested other tests to be run. Sure enough, by the end of the week, Joel was discharged—restored to health and his hearing fully intact.

The Smith's later moved to Florida. Twenty one years later, I received a phone call. It was from a young man called Joel and...you have guessed it! He wanted me to officiate at his wedding and tell the story of his personal miracle.

A number of years ago, David, my brother-in-law, was prostrated with a lower back problem. This persisted for many weeks and resulted in him being confined to bed. Eventually, the doctor booked him into Winchester hospital to undergo an operation.

My sister, Anne, phoned me the day before and asked for special prayers. It was a Sunday and I had people join hands, after evening service, to launch off our faith in the general direction of England for healing for David. The next morning, just before he was due for surgery, the pain disappeared. The presiding nurse called for the surgeon who told David to go home before he used his scalpel on him.

And home he went! He returned to work, where his colleagues gave him the sobriquet "The Miracle Man."

Thereafter, David has led walking tours all over England, plays a mean game of golf, and lives pain-free in his home in Southampton.

Once I was waiting in the medical lab for a blood sample to be taken and, lo, there was my friend Harvey and his wife. Harvey was not looking well; in fact, he had been given only a matter of weeks to live. Cancer was the problem.

I have never been reticent about where I pray, so right there in the waiting room I prayed that Doctor Jesus would touch

Harvey and grant him years of healthy living. The folk in the waiting room began to think they were in church but didn't seem to mind. Suddenly, the miracle of Hezekiah's healing came to mind. This was the account in the Bible where the prophet Isaiah spoke to the dying King and told him that the shadow on the sundial was being put back fifteen degrees— fifteen degrees, fifteen more years to live! When I spoke this to Harvey, he and his wife began to praise God. They had already been given this same prophetic word by someone else and, as far as they were concerned, the deal was sealed!

All of this was over three years ago. This past summer I saw Harvey again. He looked full of health and told me that he was hoping to go on a mission trip to Nicaragua. Not bad for a man who was given only a few weeks to live in 2011.

I was witness to a miracle more recently as well. A couple of weeks ago, my wife and I visited my daughter, Sharon, while on vacation in the lake district of Ontario. While we were relaxing by the lake shore, she remarked that her friend, who was sitting nearby, had cancer. She was a young, blonde-haired, sweet-looking lady, and what added to the tragedy of her situation was that she was a mother of four. The doctors had said that she had but a short time to live.

My daughter knows that I am likely to pray for anything that moves, so she was not surprised when I went over to introduce myself. Before I left, I laid hands on this young lady and implored that God would heal her, and that He would extend her years so that she could live to see her grandchildren. Shortly afterwards, my wife and I were on our way home.

On Sunday, August 10, 2014, I stopped in to see Sharon at her farm, just outside the city of Barrie. I was greeted by the wonderful news that her friend had phoned her, in great excitement, to say that her MRI had come back clear. The doctors are amazed. No sign of cancer!

Hallelujah! "Jesus Christ is the same yesterday, today, and forever."

"Enoch walked with God: and he was not; for God took him." (Genesis 5:24, KJV) What a great way to live and what a great way to go to be with the Lord. Let's all make that our life goal.

Ian, Wilson, Barrie, Ontario

Multiple Financial Miracles During a Health Crisis

My name is Melissa and I live in Barrie, Ontario. I'm a single mom of a beautiful daughter who is now 11 years old. God has brought me so many incredible miracles this year that I didn't know where to start.

In November 2012, I had just turned 31 years old and was diagnosed with breast cancer. At the same time, my father was also battling lung cancer and we didn't know how long he had to live. So he planned a trip for our family to go on a cruise the following January.

At the time, my cancer was already very aggressive and I thought that maybe it was too late for me to go on the trip due to the size of the tumour and the pain that I was experiencing. My life had turned upside down since hearing the word "cancer".

I work for the school board and somehow the school that I work for found out about my diagnosis and they blessed me incredibly. They gave me over one thousand dollars' worth of gift cards and over $2,500 in cash. It was such a blessing! There were also presents of all kinds being delivered to my house from everywhere and everyone. My mail box was full of surprises for several months. I didn't even have enough room to put everything. God showered me with gifts!

Then the greatest gift of all came. I own my house and was going to lose it if I didn't work two jobs. But I was in such poor health that I couldn't even work one job. My mom was taking care of my dad for he did not have long to live. Although her husband did not have a job, my middle sister quit her own job, in order to take care of me. She is my best friend, and I believe that God wanted her out of her job anyways. I feel this might have been the only way to make her see it.

One day, God whispered in my ear that I was going to be OK, even though the doctors did not know it. I had mortgage protection on my house and filled out the paper work for the benefits. Then I waited for a month and finally heard back from them. I thought the mortgage company would help me pay for my monthly mortgage payments until I was well again. But then I got something in the mail that surprised me. The letter said that they were going to pay me 287,000 dollars! I was in shock and unbelief, and had to call them to see what this meant. They told me that they were paying my whole mortgage off for me. I couldn't believe it!!! I called a friend who works at the bank and she said, "Oh my gosh; this has only happened once before!!!" This blessing was such a relief for me during my health struggles.

My family went on our vacation cruise but my dad was not well. He passed away shortly after our trip. At that time, I was so sick that I could not be there for him or spend his last hours on earth with him.

That was just the beginning of God's blessings for me. I was very sick from the chemotherapy. I had four months of treatments and lost my hair. The cancer ward gave me two grants that totalled $3,000 to put towards paying bills, and food vouchers worth $800. This paid for every single bill I had for ten months. I have never ever seen so many financial blessings in my life come so fast.

During and after the chemo, God showed me that I was going to be OK. But then I had three surgeries. The first one was in June. It took 11 hours and consisted of a double mastectomy and tummy tuck. Shortly afterwards, I was rushed to the hospital because one of my breasts was filling up with blood, and it was travelling up my arm and my neck towards my brain. I was in cardiac arrest and needed a blood transfusion. Apparently I could have died. Only three percent of people get what I had.

Yet God wanted me to live. I had amazing surgeons who were so loving, and an amazing oncologist, and incredible nurses. God was everywhere!

During the time when I was recovering in the hospital, there were so many more blessings of God. As a gift, my dentist wiped off the $300 that I owed them. I had never received child support for my 11-year-old daughter and, all of a sudden, there were $2,000 in my bank account...and then another $1,000...and this carried me through the year.

My income tax return also came in. I was told that I wouldn't be getting anything back, but I received $3,000! I was getting disability as well and was told I would be cut off in September of 2013. But God extended my time! I'm still off work and will be for the whole month of January.

My mom met an incredible man eight months after my dad passed away and she is getting married again. And I'm doing great! My hair is growing back. I'm healthy again and I'm going to live a long life. Most importantly, I'm so in love with God. I now know the glory of God and that He can do anything. Thank you, Lord, for providing for me during my illness.

Melissa Ventresca, Barrie, Ontario

God Still Does Miracles!

I will never forget it and it is important to always remember your miracles if you are blessed by God to receive one.

I was not yet a Christian and was unsure of this God guy. I had a lot of questions. How can there be a God? Why was my life such a mess right from the start? How can a child deserve to be sexually abused? Where was God then?

I spent the first 45 years of my life trying to become happy by going to therapists and self-help groups, but there was a pain so deep that nothing really helped. I also felt a lot of anger. I cried out to God many times but that was the extent of my reach.

One day, after talking with my new Christian friends, I decided to give this God thing a dedicated, serious try. I decided to go to Bible study, attend church, and pray. Approximately two weeks after this decision was made, I realized that I had not cried in a while. Where were those angry, hurt, desperate, lonely, sad feelings? I will never forget when I came to the realization that God had taken my pain away. I began to cry tears of joy, hope, love, and forgiveness as I walked with my dogs. When I looked up, I saw a perfect cloud, in a perfect blue sky, in the shape of an eye. God was speaking to my heart. He was saying, "I'm with you and I was always with you, even as a child!" I realized then that I was never alone. God was there crying with me as I was abused. I know that may sound odd, but it is such a comfort to me knowing that I was not alone.

That was six years ago and the pain has never returned. My walk with God is continuous and has been growing each and every day since then.

It was all in God's timing that I came to know Him. The surprising thing is that my daughter came to know and trust the Lord at the same time—also through new Christian friends and through the same Bible study that I happened to be attending— although several hundred kilometers away. It was called "The Truth Project".

God does still perform miracles! And the greatest miracle of all…is salvation. Thanks to my Christian friends, Sylvia and Doris, for leading me.

Lisa Zettler, Noelleville, Ontario

Truly Transformed by God's Grace

Six years ago was the beginning of my walk with Christ. Ever since I was a young girl, I can remember praying to God every night and wanting to go to church. I would beg my parents to go to church on Sunday, but I guess it was not God's timing for them just yet!

I have always been extremely close with my mother and we have been through everything together; we have been each other's support through life's obstacles. When I look back at our lives, I can see how God was at work every step of the way and how our story brings glory to Him.

The year that I moved three hours away from home, to go to university, God really began to transform my heart. He led me to the NCCF (Nipissing Canadore Christian Fellowship), where I met my future roommates and mentors. He continued to tug at my heart every day and teach me things that would transform my life.

On my first day of math class, I met a beautiful, godly woman by the name of Grace, who was instrumental in my walk with Christ. We would walk home from math class through a beautiful trail by the university in North Bay, and we would talk about God. One day, she invited me to a Bible study where we would be studying the Truth Project.

At the same time, my mom met her new friend, Sylvia, and they started walking their dogs together daily. Sylvia taught my mom about God. One day, I phoned my mom and she told me that she was attending the Truth Project Bible study as well! God must have really wanted both of us to know the truth about Him. He sure does work in mysterious ways! He transformed our hearts at the same time—while we were three hours apart and missing each other terribly. We have both grown in our faith tremendously since then, and we share Bible readings, God chats and prayers together, which has strengthened our relationship even more!

God has truly changed my life, and He has blessed me with so many amazing people who have loved me and taught me so much about the gospel. My church family has been there for me through everything and I am forever grateful. As I started to grow in my faith over the years, God challenged me with different opportunities that would draw me nearer to Him. I began to lead the prayer group in my 3rd year of university and, at the time that I was asked to do this, I had never prayed out loud in front of a group before. That quickly changed! In my 5th year, I led a Bible study with one of my dear friends.

God has been slowly transforming me every day, and now that I am finished school, I want to dedicate my career and life to Him. This past summer, my pastor had a vision of opening an arts school at our church, and he asked me if I would teach the worship dance component. I have been dancing since the age of 3 and it is a sincere passion of mine. This is another way that God has been stretching me, and I am learning so much about Him through this journey. The School of Arts was my ultimate dream and it became a reality. I am blown away every day by the Lord's goodness. I often find myself standing in the dance room at the church in complete awe of God.

I thank Him for everything that He has done in my life and my mother's life. We are living for Him and we are truly transformed!

Paige Smith, North Bay, Ontario

A Word of Knowledge Brought Peace

The year was 2008. It was the year my teenage nephew got sick—I mean REALLY sick—on death's door sick, and the doctors at Sick Kids Hospital in Toronto confirmed it. At the same time, my husband was slated to go on a big business trip to France and I had three children under the age of four to care for. I thought about what I would do all alone if my nephew didn't make it. How would I cope?

It was mid-March, on a Wednesday, and I know to pray when things get tough, and to ask others to pray with me when I need help. I knew that a good friend of mine would be volunteering at the Barrie Healing Rooms that very afternoon. From what I had heard, this was an effective Christian prayer ministry and I decided to drop in for prayer. I entered and filled out a prayer request form, but I made it really vague. I only wrote, "My nephew is sick." My friend sat in the waiting area with me while some other prayer warriors began to prepare to pray for me in the prayer room (so I KNOW that she could not possibly have given them ANY details).

When I entered the room, I was put at ease and told that the Lord had given one of the prayer team members a word for me. The word that was given was an uncommon word which nobody seemed to know the meaning of. It was the word

"RAMPART". We had to look it up in a dictionary and learned that a rampart is "an embankment encircling a castle or fort, for defense and protection against attacks, and for quick dispersing of troops.

"Does this mean anything to you?" I was asked. Well, I thought about it and then figured it might mean the Internet since we were using Facebook and email to update "our praying troops" about my nephew's condition. The prayer volunteers then prayed for me and my nephew, and I felt better leaving it in God's hands. However, I was still fretting about what to do if I need my rock of a husband in case I did have to hand my sweet nephew back to my loving God.

The very next morning, my husband emailed me his travel itinerary from France and the hotel he was to stay in was called THE RAMPART HOTEL.

Instantly, I knew that everything was going to be OK. I knew that my nephew would have the surgery he needed to live and would be fine at the end of it. I knew that I would NOT need my husband because he would be in the hotel that God had already told me about the day before.

That word of knowledge about a rampart providing protection from physical attacks made me believe that any spiritual attacks would also be stopped by God.

My nephew had the surgery he needed and was released from Sick Kids Hospital after only 6 days, although the expected recovery time given by surgeons had been 14 to 21 days. He gained back 100 pounds and also regained his faith and trust in God.

My nephew is now a strong, healthy, happy, young man in his twenties. I can't wait to see the great things God has planned for him!

Heather Hooymans, Angus, Ontario

Healing of Vertigo and Incurable Meniere's Disease

My journey began in December 2001...I think. I had experienced attacks before that, but I always blamed them on something else. At the time, I didn't know that I had a chronic illness that has no cure and gets progressively worse. I was Christmas shopping at Old Navy and, all of a sudden, I felt like I was getting the stomach flu. I managed to make it home before becoming violently sick for hours.

The next clear time that I remember, I thought I was car sick. We were driving home from Florida in 2003 and going through Bluffton, Ohio. The vertigo hit me so hard, and I was vomiting for so long, that I went into convulsions. My husband brought me to the nearest hospital (thank goodness for insurance!) and they gave me intravenous potassium to stop the convulsions. They also did numerous tests, but found nothing wrong with me. I was released in the morning and we continued on our way home.

Once we were back home in Ontario, I saw my family doctor who ordered numerous tests, ranging from vision tests to brain scans. There were still no positive results. Doctors could find nothing wrong with me. The Ear, Nose and Throat Specialist (or ENT) that I finally saw diagnosed me with vertigo migraines. Vertigo is a type of dizziness in which a patient inappropriately experiences the perception of motion (usually a spinning motion) due to dysfunction of the vestibular system in the inner ear. It is often associated with nausea and vomiting as well as a balance disorder, causing difficulties with standing or walking. I was upset. I knew that these crazy attacks, which lasted for 10 to 20 hours, weren't normal. But the attacks come in clusters; so once they went away, I felt almost normal again…at least in the beginning.

For the next few years, I would have an attack about once every few months, but I labelled them as vertigo migraines. We moved to Windsor, Ontario, in 2007. The attacks became regular by the spring of 2008. First they were weekly. Then daily! I was afraid to leave the house as these attacks were so debilitating and not pretty! My whole world would spin as if I were on a crazy CNE amusement ride. Then I would vomit for hours and hours, lying by the toilet, praying for it to stop. I was still always blaming the attacks on a migraine, possibly caused by stress. At one point that spring, it was so bad that my husband called the ambulance and I was rushed to the hospital. It was there that a doctor with no bedside manner stated to me, stone faced, "You have Meniere's disease. There is no cure. It gets progressively worse. Have a good day." And then he left. No medicine. No help. No cure!

I believe this is what really made me want to move home to Horseshoe Valley. We had been in Windsor for 14 months and I was very sick. I had no family doctor and no extended family or friends there. In addition, I was stressed as I still didn't have a full time teaching position. Basically, I was sick and lonely. I knew I had an ENT specialist and a family doctor in Barrie, so I really wanted to come home. Thankfully, God blessed me by giving my husband a clear message to come back home.

At that time, my ear, nose and throat specialist tested me and noted that I had developed tinnitus and hearing loss in my right ear. Both are clear signs of Meniere's disease. Meniere's disease is characterized by attacks that commence suddenly with violent dizziness, ringing in the ears, vomiting, a reeling sensation and unsteadiness of body equilibrium. It can be so severe that if the person does not lie down, he would fall to the floor. During the course of a severe attack, the patient is confined to bed and cannot move his head from one side to the other without experiencing disturbing sensations that the floor, bed, and chairs are turning around him. Such a bout may last several weeks before there is complete recovery. For me, the doctor prescribed a low sodium diet and Serc (an antivertigo drug). This helped me to be well for almost 2 years. I believe it was God...others claim the disease went into remission.

In the spring of 2010, I became extremely ill again, suffering daily attacks. We were in the middle of a move into a home that we were renovating. So once again, I blamed it on stress and allergies to dust. I was sick all summer and was unable to go back to work as a teacher in September. By mid-September, I was prescribed a machine called a Meniett that pushes endolymphatic fluid to the endolymphatic sac. Once again, I was well for 2 1/2 years using this machine, which most doctors saw as completely experimental. I was happy to "plug myself in" in order to feel better.

I was back to work after thanksgiving but I never felt 100%. I developed Benign Paroxysmal Positional Vertigo (BPPV). Every time I lay down, it felt like an elevator was dropping, but I was vertigo-free, so I was thankful. I would have days where I would feel "hung over" for lack of a better example, but the vertigo was gone for the most part. I was tested for allergies of various kinds, but they found none. I used the Meniett machine, took prescription medications, and tried various types of treatments, including a chiropractor, a massage therapist, a naturopath for acupuncture and herbal medicine, an osteopath, a physiotherapist, an allergy specialist, and an ENT specialist.

For the next 2 years, I was well and completely full of joy. I resumed my life with family, travel, coaching, working out, working as a teacher…and all other normal things.

Then, out of nowhere, on January 10, 2013, the vertigo hit me hard, in the middle of my class, in the computer lab. The evil one was back with a vengeance! The day before, I had been hit in the head with a basketball, but I hadn't taken notice of it. Once again, I was in a cycle of almost daily vertigo attacks. My machine wasn't helping, medicine wasn't helping, and changing my eating habits wasn't helping. I was praying and praying but I believe that God had me in this cycle for a reason. I was sick for months and months. It had never been this bad before. I had terrible thoughts that this is what my life was going to be like forever.

On Sunday, April 7, I was prayed over by members at Mosaic Church. On the following Wednesday, I visited the Barrie Healing Rooms, where the prayer team prayed for the vertigo to stop. They also included spiritual warfare prayers to get Satan out of the picture. He had been tormenting me for too long. I was also told not to blame myself for being stupid and getting that neck injury back in 2000. I sometimes felt that the vertigo could have been caused by a whiplash injury during a Phys Ed class that year. There was a blind man at the Healing Rooms that day. I prayed to God that He would heal him if He had to choose between him and me. I later realized how silly that was, because God is big enough to heal us both.

On Thursday morning, I had a major adjustment by my chiropractor. However, on my way to a Mosaic church meeting later that day, I had a major attack in the car.

On Sunday, April 14, 2013, during the Masters playoffs, I had another attack. That night, I woke up in the middle of the night and God told me about the Celebrex medication. Although I hadn't taken it since Christmas, I still had some left over; so I took it and renewed my prescription. I had received cortisone shots for my back pain and was therefore off the Celebrex for a while.

The following Wednesday, I was feeling much better but went back to the Healing Rooms for prayer again. We prayed and believed for complete healing. The message given to me that day was that I was expecting too little and that my prayers are not big enough, for nothing is impossible with our big God.

I had several doctors visits, an MRI and x-rays after this. On Tuesday, April 23, my friend, Arlene, called to invite me to go to a healing conference with her at the Hershey Centre on May 10 and 11. She told me that God had woken her up in the middle of the night and had shown her my face.

Although I had regular chiropractic adjustments, on Friday, April 26, full, violent vertigo reappeared. For several days, my head was spinning. I describe it as a "slosh head". I couldn't leave home—not even to walk the dog. At night my legs and feet would tingle, which was very uncomfortable. It could have been restless leg syndrome.

Another terrible attack occurred on May 3, at 4:00 a.m. The bathroom floor was spinning counter clockwise. In the morning, I felt as if I were "hung over". I decided to book an appointment with my doctor to get an experimental steroid shot on May 6, but he was unable to give it to me that day.

Accompanied by my friend, I attended the healing conference. I didn't receive prayer from the ministry team, but I spent a lot of time in prayer with Arlene. On Monday, May 13, the day after the Kenneth Copeland healing school, God indicated to me that He wants me to give *Him* the glory for my healing, rather than the shots I was about to receive.

I had received 3 of the 4 steroid shots that I was to get. Between shots, I felt very unsteady. I had slow, but disconcerting vertigo 3 or 4 times each week. This is normal, I was told. My head felt like there was a buzz—a vibration of sorts—on my brain, and if I moved too quickly, the vertigo would start up again. So I moved very slowly. The last 4 weeks had been very difficult. Three days after each shot, the side-effects started and made me feel very weird and off balance. My head tried to go into full vertigo, and it actually did a few times. The rest of the time, I had to lie very still for hours.

On the evening of May 31, I tried to walk around the block with my husband, Norm, but I could only make it to the corner and back. *"Soon,"* I thought, *"only two more weeks of healing, and then I should be there! I am* **expecting** *you to come, Lord, and I thank you in advance."*

Two weeks later: June 15, 2013

It had been one week since my last steroid shot. I had received one shot a week for four weeks. I was feeling well, but I still felt the symptoms lurking. The "sloshiness" was gone, but I still felt a jitter in the back of my head, like it wanted to vibrate but couldn't. I had been praying for complete healing!

Thank you, Lord, for getting me here!

On the following day, June 16, 2013, I wrote the following words: "Lord, thank you for healing me! I feel well again today and I am so thankful that you have chosen to heal me. I Praise you, Lord, for the great and mighty things you do. I praise you, God, that you have made this day. I will be glad and rejoice in it! In Jesus' name, I pray."

It's now the summer of 2014. I've learned to pray big prayers and expect great results. For the past year, I have been relatively well. I work part time and I am very tired by the afternoon. But I function almost normally. I work, I drive, I even golf again! I can't run anymore, and I haven't really worked out intensely since January 2013, but I can walk with the dog!

God has been good. I believe He wants me to remember to lean on Him so I always have a little bit of Meniere's disease with me. My neck and jaw are always sore but it is manageable. So much better than vertigo attacks!

Praise God for taking away an illness that man said had no cure!

Deb Grant, Barrie, Ontario

Jesus in Our Living Room

"For where two or three are gathered together in My name, I am there in the midst of them."

(Matthew 18:20, NKJV)

My wife, Marliene, and I are very fond of praying together, usually in the early evenings. We met to pray in our living room when we lived on Cynthia Court, in Barrie, Ontario. She sat on a chair and I sat on a footstool. I opened my Bible and declared that, since there were two of us praying in Jesus' name, that He would be with us in the Spirit. I wasn't quite prepared for what happened next!

As I was going through the long list of prayer requests, Marliene began to shake my hands forcefully. I thought to myself, *"Lord can you get her to stop; I can't concentrate with this interruption."* Marliene eventually did stop the shaking. I looked up at her and asked, "Why all the commotion?" She was very excited and shared what had happened.

As we were praying, Marliene had her eyes closed but she saw some sort of visual fluctuation, and then the living room came into view in full colour. With her head bowed and eyes closed, she could see feet in sandals to her left...then white garments. It appeared to be a man sitting in the chair to her left and, as he stood up and walked into the centre of the living room, Marliene could see that the man had white light radiating from the upper portion of his body. He turned around and raised his hands as if to bless us.

It was Jesus! He was wearing a white robe, a sash around His waist and sandals on His feet. Marliene was drawn immediately to His eyes and she felt a great peace come over her. It was as if she could look into His eyes forever—as if she were looking into eternity! She noticed what she initially thought was bad acne around His forehead. Then she realized that these were the marks left by the crown of thorns that the Romans had thrust into His head! All around His head and shoulders was a very intense white light. Marliene gazed at the Lord, and then opened her eyes. He was no longer there. She shut her eyes quickly but saw only darkness.

Marliene had a vision of Jesus standing in our living room. He was there with us in the spiritual realm, and He had opened her spiritual eyes to see Him. A rare spiritual event, but one that is cherished to this day!

Brian and Marliene Cathline, Barrie, Ontario

Healing Little Hands and Big Headaches

E arlier this evening, my three-year-old son was playing with the swivel cupboard in the kitchen as I was making dinner. When the door swung around to close, it jammed his fingers and severely pinched them. His fingers turned blue, and he was crying profusely with significant pain. I tried icing them, but it had little effect. Then I took him into the living room, sat him down, took his little hand in mine, and started praying over him, standing on the Word of God, specifically the verses of John 14:12-15. To me, the phrase "standing on" means "holding God accountable to His word." I believe it works something like this: When someone prays God's Word, God says, "Hey, angels, that's my Word; go, get it done!" Or, God performs the task directly, depending on what is being prayed.

This is the context of what I prayed: Jesus said, "Truly, truly, I say to you, he who believes in Me, the works that I do, he will do also; and greater works than these he will do; because I go to My Father. Whatever you ask in My name, that will I do, so that the Father may be glorified in the Son. If you ask Me anything in My name, I will do it" (John 14:12-14, NKJV).

My actual prayer went something like this: "I know, Jesus, that my little boy will be healed instantly, and his pain will be removed instantly, if it is the Father's will, and I stand on your Word, and trust that healing this little boy, falls under the Father's will. Be healed, son, in Jesus' name. Pain leave in Jesus' name". As soon as I stopped praying, my little son looked at me and his crying ceased. I asked him, "Do your fingers hurt?" He replied, "No, daddy!" I continued, "Let me see your hand." I took his hand and saw that his fingers were completely healed. I was actually a bit startled, but not surprised. Then I said, "Son, you are healed! Jesus healed you," and he gave me a big high five—with the hand that had just been healed.

Release from Migraines

A Christian woman I was dating had a severe migraine headache. She had the curtains closed so that no light could get into the house. I sensed this was an attack by Satan and his fallen angels, so I asked her if it would be okay for me to lay my hands on her forehead and pray. She replied, "Yes". Rather than praying for healing, as in the healing that my son had experienced, I felt this time I needed to use the power and authority that Jesus gives us in Luke 10:19—that is, the authority "to trample on snakes and scorpions" (meaning on Satan and his fallen angels). I laid my hand on her forehead, and reminded the enemy that this woman is a child of God, that he has no rights over her, that her body is a holy temple for the Holy Spirit, and that he has no right to harm her. I said, "Satan, you must release in Jesus' name. Migraine, release in Jesus' name. Satan, let go of her, in Jesus' name. I cover you, Satan, in the blood of Jesus." I could feel her forehead twitch each time I went after the enemy in Jesus' name, and sensed the enemy was releasing. I reminded the enemy that he MUST obey. After a few minutes of going after Satan in Jesus' name, I asked her to open her eyes, and she couldn't believe it—the migraine went from 10 out of 10 on the pain scale, down to 2 out of 10. She wanted to stop at that point, but I said, "No way, it must leave completely." So, using Jesus' power and authority, I went back into warfare once more, removing any little tentacles remaining attached to her. The migraine was healed! I spoke in Jesus' name, and it was done!

On another occasion, a female friend, who had recently become a Christian, was to go to church on a Wednesday evening. I was to pick her up. I called and she sounded sick. She had a migraine headache. It was already 5:00 p.m. and we needed to leave by 6:30. She didn't want to go. I sensed this was an attack from Satan to keep her from going to church, especially since she was a brand new Christian. I asked her to please push through this, no matter how hard it may be, and come to church. I promised her that this migraine would be 100% gone before she walks in through the church doors. She agreed to come. On the way, while driving, I was having thoughts like "*No way is her headache going to go away.*" I was feeling fear, anxiety, and all kinds of weird, negative emotions. I realized where these thoughts were coming from, but I didn't speak out loud about any of it because I didn't want the enemy to know that I knew he was doing this. When we got to the church parking lot, I asked my friend how her headache was, and she said it was still a 10 out of 10. I asked if it would be okay for me to lay my hands on her forehead, and she agreed. I prayed exactly the same as in the testimony above and had the same results. The migraine headache was 100% cured! Also, all the negative thoughts and feelings that had been placed on me by Satan while driving had left. I knew for certain that this attack was to keep this new Christian from going to church.

More recently, I saw another headache healed by using the authority of Jesus. It was for a Christian customer of mine. I prayed for him and when he opened his eyes, he simply said, "Wow, it's gone!"

There is so much power given to Christians by Jesus. If Christians understood how to use the power Jesus gave us, and if they had the wisdom to know when to pray for healing and when to go after Satan and his fallen angels, this world would be a different place. I pray that Christians would wake up and stop sleeping; that they would use their power and authority, and pray for the wisdom to know how to use it.

Shawn Thompson, Barrie, Ontario

The Miracle of Forgiveness That Set Me Free

Three words describe my childhood: fear, anger, and heartache. I remember being 10 years old and having thoughts of ending my life. There were times when the pain was so great I literally thought that my chest would burst open! Why? Why was I so full of fear? Why was there so much pain in my heart? Why was I angry a lot of the time?

Many, many, many times I cried out to God for answers. I longed to know His love and to be free of the fear, the anger and the pain that threatened to overwhelm me. When I was alone, I cried buckets of tears. The Bible says that God collects all our tears in a bottle. Mine must have been a B- I- G bottle!

I felt so alone…so unloved…so confused!

Eventually, God began showing me the reason for all the pain, fear, and anger, and He began to bring understanding. In dreams, in visions, and in impressions, He let me see a little bit into the memories that were buried deep inside of me. Things began to make sense. But most importantly, He gave me hope. You see, there were many, many times I thought and felt like giving up—calling it quits—like I was at the end of my rope. I'm not sure exactly when it first happened, but one day God showed me a picture of myself. In that picture, I was free! I was well! I had peace and was full of joy! And that picture kept me going, kept me pressing more and more into Him...my Healer.

It took years and years! I went to counselor after counselor, church after church, seeking help, seeking healing. Every time I felt like giving up, there was that picture again! It was like a light at the end of the tunnel of darkness I was living in. I wanted to be free! I wanted to feel loved! I wanted to experience joy in my life!

I began forgiving the people in my life who had hurt me. I repented for my sin. I was delivered from a spirit of death. But I still wasn't free. There was one person I was having trouble forgiving. Oh, I knew that God instructs us to forgive, and I spoke the words of forgiveness many times. But, for some reason, the breakthrough that I wanted and needed wasn't happening. I didn't know what else to do. Earlier on, I had forgiven someone who took advantage of me when I was a child and I literally felt a release in my body. I **knew** that I had forgiven him. I was able to bless him and have not had any hard feelings towards him since then. But with this other person, I wasn't experiencing that kind of release.

I experienced a lot of sickness as a child and into my adult years. Not sickness that kept me in bed, but an almost constant awareness of not feeling well. One night, I invited a few people from our church to come pray for me, as the Bible instructs when one is sick. I was sick of not feeling well! The people in our church prayed for me many times. I didn't know it, but this night was to be a turning point in my life. While praying for me, one of the women whispered to me, "Have you forgiven _____?" I responded to her, "I've tried. I've spoken the words of forgiveness but I haven't felt a release." She said, "You need to forgive him." In my heart, I began crying out to God to help me forgive completely.

The next day was a Saturday and I felt compelled to spend time alone with God. I asked my husband to look after our daughter so I could be alone with God. I went to our bedroom and closed the door. After flopping down on the bed, I turned my heart to the Lord and admitted that I needed His help to totally forgive this man for hurting me as a child. He was someone I was supposed to be able to trust; someone who should have been protecting me, not harming me—someone I should have been able to look up to. What he did to me was downright cruel and disgusting! But I had to forgive him. I had to let him go if I wanted to be free like the woman I saw in the picture.

I didn't know how to let go in this situation. I didn't know what to do differently. But God knew what was needed and, that morning, He let me see a little bit of what hell was like. It was awful! In response, I cried out, "Oh God! I don't want my worst enemy to have to go there!" Miraculously, in that moment, my heart released this man. You see, the person I needed to forgive had died many years ago. The fear in my heart was, *"what if he is in heaven?"* I didn't particularly want to see him again. But then the tears began to flow down my face—tears of release, tears of forgiveness, cleansing tears that turned into tears of joy as the weight I had carried for over 30 years lifted off me. I instantly experienced a freedom that I had never known before. Joy began to explode in me and I also felt a peace that I had never known.

I knew the forgiveness was now complete and I thanked God for His faithfulness towards me. I thanked Him for not giving up on me. To this day, I thank Him for the miracle of forgiveness. My life has forever been changed and now, 14 years later, after more healing and finally being able to experience the Father's love for me, I am living the life of freedom, of wholeness, and of joy that I saw in the picture of the woman that God gave me years ago. I am forever grateful to our miracle-working God who loves me so very, very much!

Carol Weber, Moorefield, Ontario

Died but Came Back To Life

My name is Aurele Le Breton and I'm a believer in a big God—a God of healing, truth and MIRACLES. I was born and raised in New Brunswick, in a small town by the name of Bellefond. I worked as a lumberjack, and was bound by drinking and drugs. In 1988, I received Jesus into my life and never turned back. I now live in the small town of Lefroy, Ontario, which is south of Barrie, by Lake Simcoe— only a five minute walk to the lake. I have been the owner of my own home renovation business for about 18 years now.

I've been married for 23 years to my lovely wife, Linda, and we have pastored and ministered to youth, young adults, and adults, moving in the prophetic and healing by the power of the Holy Spirit. We have traveled to West Africa, the Philippines, and other Third World countries. God has changed me and my whole life is now offered up for Him to work through me, in order to lead people to Christ and to allow signs and wonders to follow me for the benefit of others.

I also have a recent miracle story to tell you about myself. It happened on March 30, 2014. I have been running for about five years now and have been doing very well. I have been running 5 km, 10 km, 16 km, and half-marathons of 21.1 km, and I've also tackled the 30 km run twice, in Hamilton, Ontario. On March 30th of this year, I was doing the 30 km run for the second time, and it was a good run at that. I finished the race with no problems and made it in good time. We all ran OK with the group, said our goodbyes, and were ready to head home.

My wife, our good friend Geoff, and I got into my truck. Geoff had run beside me for half of the distance, but then had to slow down. Anyway, we got to my truck and started on our way home. Then I realized that we were going the wrong way because we needed to drop Geoff off at his truck, which he had left at the hotel where we had stayed the night before. We turned to head up around the upper James area, going up a hill. As I was driving up this hill, I started to have some kind of indigestion and, at the same time, I saw a fire truck in front of us. Traffic was bumper to bumper, and a small voice within me said, *"Tell them to stop the fire truck."* But of course, I kept driving, not saying anything out loud. I slowly started to pass the fire truck and the pain got stronger, and again the small voice said, *"Tell them to stop the fire truck."* Again I kept driving, not saying anything. At that moment, both Linda and Geoff looked at me and asked, "Are you alright?" Hearing that still small voice once more, I replied, "No, not really. Can you stop that fire truck?"

Linda told Geoff to jump out of the truck to ask them to help me. At that time, we were at a set of traffic lights, so I made a right turn and the fire truck turned behind me. The firemen put me on the tailgate of my truck and gave me some oxygen so I could breathe better. All of a sudden, an ambulance came around the corner with its lights on. The two attendants jumped out of the ambulance and asked, "Where is the fire?" One of the firemen said, "We never called for a fire or for any assistance, but we are sure glad you're here. You guys can take over." So two young paramedic ladies took over with the oxygen and put me in the ambulance. I was feeling pretty good at this point, and they even told me not to worry. They told Linda and Geoff to follow us to the hospital, which was only ten minutes away. They didn't even put the sirens on.

When we arrived at the hospital emergency area, the driver of the ambulance came around to open the two back doors, while joking with her friend. At that same moment, I passed out.

The paramedics pulled me out to start CPR, but it was not working for them. They couldn't revive me at this point, so my heart stopped. I was dead! Right away, they started using the defibrillation paddles—once—twice—and the third time they got my heart going again. The doctors said that I was dead for just under 3 minutes and they weren't going for the fourth shot!

While I was dead, I had a vision come to me. In this vision, I was driving my GMC truck and I saw myself crashing if I closed my eyes. So I kept my eyes open wide and that felt good. All of a sudden, I saw myself lying on a bed, very relaxed, and within seconds, my nephew, Uriel, appeared beside my bed. He was talking to me but I couldn't hear him. I realized what he was saying to me by reading his lips: "Uncle, I'm not letting you go through or go by. You can't go now because you have too much to do, and too many people to talk to. No, you're not going; you're staying…" and so on. At that moment, I started to come to. I was back in the room where there were about 9 or 10 people working on me.

I was alive again and talking to the doctors, answering all their questions properly. They were all amazed by how I pulled through so fast, but they knew I needed an operation right away. They gave me some medication to make me drowsy. Then they went ahead and installed a stent on the artery, at the entrance of the heart. The doctors later told me that my artery was 99% blocked by plaque, due to stress and eating red meat. My recovery was "a miracle", as the doctors put it. They told me that I would need to recover at the hospital for a good week because of the type of heart attack I had, and because of the stent that they put in. Shortly after my operation, doctors were surprised at what they were seeing. I was sitting up and talking. The nurses said, "This is unbelievable." I was already walking around the day after the operation, and I had a clean slate for all the tests they did on me. I had been admitted on Sunday, late afternoon, and they already released me on Tuesday afternoon to go home and rest. The doctors and the medical team were astonished and had no reason to keep me in the hospital. They said that they had never seen anything like this before.

A quick recovery or a miracle such as mine is often the result of people praying—like my faith-filled wife Linda, my pastor from Jubilee Celebration Centre, all the people from my church, and my family and friends from all over. Knowing that these wonderful people were praying for me brought me peace and a quick recovery. When Linda first heard that I went into cardiac arrest, she came into the emergency entrance, but she was only shocked for a few moments. Then the Holy Spirit softly spoke to her: "It's going to be OK. Aurele is going to be alright. It's not his time yet." At that moment, Linda felt the presence of the Holy Spirit come over her, giving her a sense of peace. I believe that prayers are powerful in times like this, so never give up on your prayers for your loved ones.

I know that I serve a big God—the God who created all things, who knew me from the beginning and will know me to the end. God knows all about us and loves us, so He sent His Son, Jesus Christ, to die on the cross for us—for me and for all of you who want to receive Him as your Lord and Saviour. I encourage you to repent of your sins, turn to Him, and He will forgive you. Accept Him into your life as your Lord and Saviour if you haven't already done so.

Now to recap briefly how God was present in this situation: My heart was in great shape because I was a runner and I've had lots of training. My friend, Geoff, was with us the day of my heart attack. If he hadn't been with us, I would have taken a different route home. The fire truck happened to be in front of us, in a traffic jam, to slow us down. My wife asked me at the last moment, before the lights turned, if I was ok. The two attendants with the ambulance came around the corner instantly, without the firemen having called them. We were very near to one of the best hospitals in Canada that treats heart patients. I saw my nephew in a vision at the same time that he was driving through a big snow storm, in New Brunswick, to go to his mom and dad's. He said he had to hold the steering wheel really tight to keep his truck on the road at the exact time that I had the heart attack. I had a really quick recovery at the hospital, as confirmed by doctors.

I would say to you that God had His hand on me, that He has a great plan for my life, and He didn't want it to be cut short. He has a great plan for your life as well. I know that I have a great heavenly Father, His great Son, and the great Holy Spirit to comfort me and guide me throughout my walk with Him. In the valley of death and at the top of the mountains, He is always there.

In John 14:1-6, Jesus said, "Let not your heart be troubled; you believe in God, believe also in me. In my Father's house are many mansions; if it were not so, I would have told you. I go to prepare a place for you. And if I go and prepare a place for you, I will come again and receive you to myself; that where I am, there you may be also...I am the way, the truth, and the life. No one comes to the Father except through me."

Give Jesus a chance to make a difference in *your* life.

Aurele Le Breton, Lefroy, Ontario

Trusting a Faithful God

It is easy to say we trust God to provide for us when we have a regular pay cheque or income, but when the jobs we have bring in less than enough to pay even the basic bills...and then we have a minor accident in which our car becomes a write-off...the challenge to trust is on.

That's where I found myself in September 2013. But the Lord had prepared me for this. Ever since God had called my sister and me to sell our home-baking business and follow Him, He taught us "to seek first the kingdom of God and His righteousness, and all these things will be added unto you." It had been a walk of faith. At first we had money in savings, but we felt prompted, from time to time, to help out others in the body of Christ who were in need, and eventually the savings were used up.

The Lord provided several cleaning jobs for us almost immediately, but that was it. It seemed to be a time when the Lord wanted us to spend time with Him, learning His ways and the ways of His kingdom. To earn our daily bread by the sweat of our brows is not the way of His kingdom. That came as a result of sin, but in the beginning it was not so. God desires a Father-son or Father-daughter relationship with us, His children.

The day I lost my car, I was reminded of the words that I had been declaring regularly. "I am always at the right place at the right time, because my steps are ordered by the Lord." I chose to believe and declare that it was true, even in this circumstance. When condemning thoughts came, telling me that I was too occupied with a business venture that I had just started, the Lord spoke to me and said, "No, this was all in my plan." What a loving Daddy we have! He sees the big picture; He knows the connections that He wants to make.

Up until that time, I had been living in Elmira but I was going elsewhere to Bible study, church, and prayer meetings. Now that I no longer had a car, I couldn't travel freely. One Saturday evening, the Lord prompted me to attend a praise and worship night at a fellowship close to my home. Connections were made and I knew that I had a calling there. "God moves in mysterious ways, His wonders to perform..."

At the time my car was taken, I was worse off financially than I had ever been before, and my sister, who had been helping me with my payments, was also between jobs. I knew it was out of the question to think of purchasing another car, unless the Lord provided supernaturally. I believed that He would do it in His time. But I didn't know how He would do it, or when.

One day, as I was spending time with the Lord, listening to a message on the Father's heart of love, the words of Jesus came to me. I thought about the passage where He said that earthly dads won't give their children stones when they ask for bread. He went on to say that "If you, being evil, can give good gifts to your children, how much more will your heavenly Father give good gifts to His children?" I recalled how a friend of mine had given a car to his daughter. I wept as I realized, like never before, that God is, indeed, my heavenly Daddy, and that

He wants to and will give me, His daughter, a car in His time. His timing is always perfect.

At one point a friend gave me $200, saying God told her that she's to tell me it's for me. I was not to give it away. When I asked the Lord what I am to do with it, He said, "Put it in your savings as seed for the car." So that's what I did. Two months after losing my car, I was given a cheque of $2000 to use towards another car. The Lord had multiplied that seed money by 10! That's the God I serve! I'm still believing for that cheque of $20,000, and then of $200,000. God wants to bless His children, but we have to come into alignment with His plans and purposes, or else we'll use what He gives us on ourselves and forget our God who gives us the power to get wealth.

The Lord provided a car for slightly less than the $2000. He is blessing it, and I know that He will continue to provide what is needed to keep it on the road. He is a faithful God and I am falling in love with Him more and more.

Malinda Bowman, Elmira, Ontario

Faith Comes By Hearing

I was born in 1949 into a family in which members on my mother's side all experienced serious hearing problems. My grandmother used a device that looked like a horn, the slim end of which needed to be inserted into the outer ear canal. My mother and two sisters were also hard of hearing but used progressively better hearing aids. I've been wearing a hearing aid since the age of 18.

A few years back, a Christian friend visited my home and suggested that prayers may alleviate my hearing difficulties. I admit that I was skeptical. Several months later, the same friend noticed that I was not wearing my hearing aid, a device that I loathed to wear because it made my world so loud. Hearing aids do not filter out human voices and make all other noises recede somewhat. I preferred my silent world. I tried to get by with lip-reading.

Needless to say, my hearing impediment often produced awkwardness through serious misunderstandings. Some of these situations made me feel so ashamed; I sometimes wished to sink into a hole never to resurface. Here's an example. During an award ceremony at my children's elementary school, I thought I had heard my name called. I walked up to receive the award only to be told it wasn't for me but for somebody else.

However, more and more I began to notice that these embarrassing situations became less and less frequent. Only then did the possibility dawn on me that I might, indeed, have regained hearing. But I still dismissed the idea outright.

During a chance meeting, when my Christian friend mentioned that she still prays for me, I shyly admitted that I haven't worn my hearing aid in many weeks—even months.

I told her that one day, on my way to work, I realized that I had forgotten my hearing aid at home. If I had taken the time to return home to get it, I would have been late for work. Reluctantly, I decided to go without it. That day, I became aware of the fact that I could hear what the children in my classroom were saying, even without the hearing device. I was surprised and pleased.

These days I am convinced that my friend's prayers were answered. I am deeply grateful for her continuous prayers for me. I enjoy the sounds of my grandchildren talking, the birds singing in the early morning sunshine, and the wind rustling through the tree branches. I can even hear the door of a car parked across the street slam shut.

I also believe in paying good deeds forward. I became involved in my church in many volunteer positions, including serving as committee secretary, taking notes of what is discussed and resolved during the meetings. All this without the aid of an assistive hearing device. Praise God!

"So faith comes from hearing, that is, hearing the Good News about Christ." (Romans 10:17, NLT)

Heidi Minuti, Angus, Ontario

No More Cane!

I have been experiencing pain in my upper leg for many years and have had much prayer for healing. I had my first x-ray in 2008. Ever since then, the pain has been getting worse at the top of my right leg hamstring, under my right "cheek". I've had therapy, massage, laser, and acupuncture, but nothing seemed to work. Finally I had an MRI, early in 2013. It showed an apparent tear in my right side hamstring tendon.

Having lived with pain for years limited my mobility and it was difficult for me to keep up our family home. One cold and snowy day, in the month of February, we thought we should move to Barrie, closer to our daughter. When Ruth, our daughter, heard this, she was thrilled. We decided to put our house up for sale and hoped to find a small apartment, where maintenance would be taken care of by the building management. Our house sale and the purchase of our condo was a miracle. Christ really directed us in our move.

We chose a Christian friend, whom we knew from a church that we had attended, as our realtor. Before we knew it, we were packing to prepare for the staging. Our realtor friend took us to see a condo. Instantly we loved it and knew it was for us. We knew nothing about condos, but God did! We put an offer in on it. Immediately we got an offer on our house too! It was adjusted to please us and on March 16, the next day, we left for sunny Florida. We took my walker and a cane with us because of my sore leg.

We had some problems while we were in Florida and flew home sick on April 4. We got possession of our condo on April 12 and, with the help of our daughter, we moved to Barrie on April 29.

We were fortunate enough to get a lovely unit that faces south. It is sunny and warm, and we get free heat from the sun when it's shining. The size is wonderful and everything about it is amazing. It's a miracle how it all happened so fast and so perfectly. God was definitely in on the planning because we could never have planned it like this. He directs and guides even where we live and how we live. Last year, we hadn't even thought about a move. God knew it was time, even though we didn't!

The pain in my upper leg was still very bad throughout the summer. I took pain pills that did not help and had prayer a number of times.

I was booked for an injection early in October. By then, I was having some good days, free of pain, during the day. Upon hearing this, the doctor at Royal Victoria Hospital in Barrie decided that the injection might irritate the situation even more and he decided not to give the needle.

Since then, I have not needed my cane. Praise the Lord! Upon rising in the morning, it is slow to release, but within about 30 minutes, it clears up and the pain is gone. All we can do is thank the Lord for whatever happened. We don't need to understand—we just need to trust Him. Nothing is impossible with God. No more cane for me!

We praise the Lord daily for guiding us in our move and thank Him for my healing.

Gen Whyte, Barrie, Ontario

Believe and Receive

Hebrews 11:1 says, "Now faith is the substance of things hoped for, the evidence of things not seen."

At the age of thirty, my husband and I gave our hearts to the Lord and we were saved. At this point in my life, I was not physically well. A short while later, we became very involved in the Baptist church we attended. We joined the choir, taught Sunday school, worked in Pioneer Girls, and sponsored the young people's group for five years. We had forty teenagers in our home every Friday night. Needless to say, my health was suffering. My spiritual life was spent more on works than on learning the Word of God. Yes, I knew Jesus healed people in the Bible, but I did not hear much preached about it from the pulpit.

Not long after this, I was diagnosed with a blood disease called sickle-cell anemia. My prayer to God was, "I know you can heal people; please heal me." My treatment for this disease started with injections in my arm and iron injections in my hip. I was also taking two blood pills a day.

My husband, who was an attorney, was offered a business opportunity and we therefore moved to Gettysburg, PA, in 1978. Once we were settled there, my husband found a church called Four Square Gospel, which turned out to be Pentecostal. We fell in love with the people, the pastor, and the Good News that was preached there.

Several weeks later, we joined the Gettysburg Country Club. While swimming at the pool one Saturday, a woman approached us and introduced herself as Madeline Desonia, from New York. She asked, "Didn't I see you last Sunday at Four Square Church?" We replied, "Yes!" She added, "It's nice to see you," and walked away.

The following Wednesday I was at the pool and ran into Madeline again. We talked and I shared about my illness with her. She was shocked and asked me, "Have you not asked Jesus to heal you?" My reply was, "Lots of times, but nothing happened, so I stopped asking.

"Nonsense," she said. "Have you heard of Women Aglow?"

"No," I replied.

She firmly said, "Fine, I'm going to take you to a meeting at the Fire Hall on Saturday night. There's a woman speaker from Michigan. She is conducting a healing service."

I flatly said, "No thanks. I'm going to the hospital Friday for my tests and I won't feel up to it."

Again she said, "Nonsense! You're coming with me. I'll pick you up at 6:30 p.m." Then she left.

Later that evening, I went to bed early and decided to read what we had been discussing at the pool. It was 1st Peter, chapter 2, verse 24: By Jesus' stripes ye **were** healed. While pondering this verse over and over, I discovered the key word was **"were"**. Not "going to be healed," but "were healed"—past tense! And, as I was pondering, I was startled by an audible voice, saying, "Go for your tests next Monday." Startled as I was, I looked around, expecting to see my husband, but no one was there.

I called out, "Gary!" But there was no answer. I passed it off and kept reading. Approximately fifteen minutes went by and I heard the same voice with the same words, "Go for your tests next Monday." Thinking that this was my husband, playing a joke, I yelled, "Gary, I know it's you!" There was no response. I got out of bed, looked around, and found no one upstairs.

I went back to bed and continued reading. Again the same voice with the same words appeared. This time, I threw on my dressing gown and flew downstairs, only to find my husband reading in his study.

I said, "This isn't very funny, Gary."

He had no idea what I was talking about. When I explained, he replied, "I think the Lord is trying to tell you something."

I didn't sleep much that night and my spirit kept saying that something good is going to happen. After changing my appointment at the hospital, I called Madeline and told her that I would be ready for her to pick me up.

So off we went to the meeting that Saturday night. I was so excited I couldn't sit still while the lady was speaking. The healing service was about to begin and I was ready. I knew that God was going to heal me. When I was taken to the lady speaker, Madeline explained the situation about the disease I was suffering with. Physically, I did not look well. My lips were purple, my skin was too white, and my eyes were black.

The lady said, "Joan, I'm going to ask you three questions, anoint you with oil, and then lay hands on you and pray."

"Number one: Do you believe God wants you sick?"

My reply was, "No."

"Number two: Do you believe Jesus heals today?"

My reply was, "Yes."

"Number three: Do you believe you're going to be healed now?"

My reply was, "Yes."

"That's all I want to hear," she said. She called for pastors in their seats to come up and bring oil. I was then asked to raise my hands unto the Lord and repeat: "I believe, Lord, you healed me 2000 years ago on Calvary. I take and receive my healing **now**. By Jesus' stripes, I am healed." And with that, I went down under the power of the Holy Spirit!

I could hear people in a far off place, shouting, "Praise God; praise God!" When I was assisted back up to my feet, to my amazement, Madeline was screaming, "Look at her face!" My lips were pink, my face was rosy, and there were no more black eyes. It was a glorious sight.

The manifestation of healing was there but now came the victory. I entered the hospital the following Monday morning for my usual tests. Three days later, I received a call from the hospital lab, asking me to come in again. Somehow, the lab in Virginia had sent back wrong test results. I went in again and had more blood taken. Three days after that, there was another call. The same problem…the same results.

I went back again to be tested and this time, three days later, I received a call from Dr. Cohen's office, the Head Hematologist in the hospital, who was also my personal doctor.

When I arrived at her office, she was sitting behind her desk, glasses down on her nose, looking at me very skeptically. The silence was deadening. She then spoke. "What is going on?"

I said, "Excuse me?"

She repeated, "What is going on?"

After a moment, I said, "Dr. Cohen, I know you are Jewish and don't believe that Jesus is the Messiah, but I am a Christian and Jesus has healed me."

She was silent for a moment. Then she rose from her desk, came over to me, put her hands on my shoulder and said, "I knew something was happening, but I wasn't sure what it was. Your blood test came back from the lab in Virginia all three times reporting your blood to be pure and perfect." Then Dr. Cohen added, "Joan, I wasn't going to tell you until later that you would not live out this year, but it looks like your Jesus had a different plan in mind."

This was in 1978. I am now 77 years of age and still going strong for my Lord. Praise Jesus! Since then, I've taken no pills and no injections. I began to study faith.

I asked the Lord, "Father, why did you not heal me all those years ago when I asked you to?"

He said, "I did. It was done 2000 years ago on Calvary, but you didn't have any faith." Then He said, "Listen to your words: 'Jesus, I'm sick. Please heal me.' Jesus did heal you 2000 years ago, but you didn't take your healing by faith. I'm a faith God. Faith is **now**. All you had to do was receive it and take it. You were waiting on me and I was waiting on you!"

"Jesus answered and said unto them, 'Ye do err, not knowing the scriptures, nor the power of God.'"

Believe and receive. Mark 11:24

Stand in Faith. James 1:6

And all the glory goes to God!

Joan Martin, Barrie, Ontario

I Believe!

In 2003, my immune system completely shut down and I was very sick. Prior to this shutdown, I had issues with my bowels off and on, but since I had been on a prescription drug called Prednisone most of my adult life, this steroid masked the problems.

In 2007, I went off Prednisone for 3 months to see what would happen. I was still not well and, in September 2007, I was diagnosed with severe colitis. Colitis refers to an inflammation of the colon or large intestine. Doctors did 15 biopsies and all 15 were infected. On a good day, I may have gone to the bathroom 20 to 30 times; on a bad day (or several bad days), I would have to go up to 40 or 50 times. You can imagine the effects this had on my body. Then my doctor prescribed a medication called Pentasa, which gave me back some quality of life. At this point, I had a few more good days than bad.

In the meantime, if there were any Christian healing services going on in our area, my husband, Bernard, and I would go. On one occasion, we went to a service at Timothy Christian School. A man asked if there was anything in particular that I needed prayer for and, because I wanted to hear from God, I said, "No." The man started to pray and he prayed for my lower extremities. He also said that he believed I would be healed and that I would be a testimony to my family and friends.

From January to April 2010, I had another severe colitis flare up. I went back on Prednisone for a month but found no relief. I made an appointment with my doctor and was prescribed another steroid, specifically for the bowel, which provided absolutely no relief. Then I visited an endocrinologist and he put me on yet another prescription that was 15 times more powerful than Pentasa, called Mezavant. About 3 weeks later, I started feeling better and stayed that way until the fall. But I started noticing small changes in my body, making me feel out of sorts, to the point that I thought I was losing my mind. My family doctor couldn't "see" anything wrong and suggested that, if things didn't improve, maybe a small dose of antidepressant would be the answer. I left his office very discouraged.

In the spring of 2011, I went to work one day and started feeling horrible and began vomiting. Bernard and my daughter had to come and bring me home. By the time we arrived home, I was still vomiting and was unable to walk upstairs. My mind was filled with horrible memories of being so severely sick, just like when my immune system shut down. I started crying as the fear of "what if" came over me.

Bernard called some prayer warriors from our church and they came over to pray with me. We went through some inner healing issues, using the "Restoring the Foundations" teachings, and GOD showed up! When we were finished praying, I was able to stand, come downstairs, talk and laugh. In the days that followed, the Lord gave me insight into the medication I was on, and it turns out that I had 12 out of 20 possible side effects for this medication. Right then, I took a step of faith and went off the medication. I had no colitis flare ups and I just kept praising and thanking Jesus. I am now eating foods that I normally could never eat, without negative results, and I have not taken any medications for colitis since April 2011. I believe I am healed.

2014 update: I don't just "believe" I am healed…it's been 3 years now and I KNOW I AM HEALED from all symptoms of colitis. I continue to eat foods that I couldn't eat before and I am feeling great! PRAISE JESUS!

Sonia Allain, Angus, Ontario

Nothing Is Too Hard For Him

May I tell you that the Father is still in the miracle business today?

In November 2007, I went to the hospital for routine sinus surgery. During the operation, my skull was accidently hit and a small hole resulted. Unfortunately, no one realized what had happened. The surgery continued on as normal and I was sent home a few hours later.

During the night my head started aching, and by morning I could hardly stand the pain. I had only just become a Christian about 6 months previous; so it didn't really dawn on me to pray. My husband took me back to the hospital the next morning, where we were told that "Yes, indeed, sinus surgery is painful for some; so go home, rest, and take over the counter headache pills for the pain." So home we went!

By the next morning, the headache had become so bad that I was passing out. My husband called an ambulance and I was taken back to the hospital again, only to be sent home a second time. I was told that I had to give it time to heal.

The rest of the day and night were horrendous and I don't remember much about it. My husband said that, by now, I couldn't stand any kind of light in the room and my neck and shoulders were becoming stiff. My husband therefore called for another ambulance. This time, I was very sick and the doctors had no answers as to why.

No one knew what to do or how to help me. A nurse who had taken me to another area of the hospital for a CAT scan realized that, during the short time I was getting the scan, I had become much worse and was now very close to death. My family was asked if they wanted clergy to be called but, being non-Christian, they declined. I believe the Lord had been watching over me but this was the point where the Lord intervened!

The nurse was the first to recognize the signs that it may be bacterial meningitis. They called in an infectious disease specialist. He did a spinal tap and confirmed that's what I had. But no-one had any idea how I had contracted it. At this point, I had been sick for 4 1/2 days. Doctors said that I should have been dead by now!

They started me on medications and moved me upstairs where I could be isolated. It was a few hours later that my husband told me I "woke up" and told him not to look at the walls. I said that Satan had written something in red and if he read it, it would hurt him and me. Of course, he looked at the wall and couldn't see anything, but apparently I could. When the nurse came in, I seemingly told her the same thing. My husband said I was panicking and I asked him to call my daughter. I told him to ask her to go on my Facebook page and look for a specific lady from church that I had become Facebook friends with, just the day before my operation. I said to tell her what was happening and that I needed my new friend to pray for the armour covering for me. The wonderful thing about this conversation was that I had no knowledge of saying any of these things, nor did I have any idea what the "armour covering" was. My daughter followed through right away and my new friend prayed for the armour of God to cover me and got the prayer chain praying as well.

As you can guess, things happened quickly after that. They found the hole in the skull, and I was transported to a Toronto Hospital where they operated on me. Everything worked out very well. Apparently no one should survive having bacterial meningitis as long as I had it, but here I am, and I give all the praise to the Lord for this miracle. Without Him orchestrating all the pieces together, I would not be here today, and I thank Him for watching over me and keeping me safe.

This is not quite the end of the story though. During this scary ordeal, I lost my sense of taste and smell. I also went through a time, on and off, where my mind became foggy and I would lose words and had a lot of memory loss. Whether this was because of the meningitis or the operation was not known, but it was a small price to pay for my life—which leads me to the second part of this wonderful story.

For the past six and a half years, I've thanked God for the miracle He accomplished by saving me from death due to the meningitis. But I also knew that He could restore my taste and smell because He's the Great Physician and nothing is too hard for Him to accomplish. I have been taught that you pray for something just once and then praise the Lord for the miracle of answered prayer. So I have been praising Him every day just waiting for Him to fix me. Never once did I give up hope that He would heal me. I knew that if I didn't receive the healing on this earth, then I would be healed in heaven; but I just felt that it would be on this earth.

One day I was praising Him and something "clicked". I knew, that I knew, that I knew! I thanked Him for the miracle He was going to accomplish and then I waited, in anticipation, still praising Him. Of course, my loving Father came through. One day, about two weeks after the "click", at the end of February 2014, I walked into a public bathroom (yup, God does have a sense of humour) and I wondered what was different. And then it hit me—it was the bathroom smell! Yes, you bet I praised the Lord! Later I went into a coffee shop and, hallelujah, I smelled the coffee. What a wonderful smell! Later that night, I took a bite of a banana and almost spit it out because I thought it was bad. Then I realized it was because it actually had a taste! That was almost a month ago, and I am so happy to say that I smell and taste everything now.

I was very blessed with that miracle. But then God went one step further and, within a few days, the fog lifted and my memory and words became clear. It dawned on me that I hadn't been praying for my memory to come back. I have no idea why, but He gave me that gift anyway. I can now think, speak, read, and do all sorts of things that I haven't been able to do properly over the past six and a half years. Isn't our Father awesome?

I am writing this story to tell people to never, never give up! Our Father is a wonderful "Dad" who only wants the best for us. He wants our cup to not only be full, but to be overflowing. I don't know why I had to go through what I did, but it doesn't matter because He knows the reason and that's good enough for me. The following is the ending to a poem I once wrote and I would like to pass it along to others because it has helped me during the tough times in my journey…

"The Lord, in all His wisdom,

has a purpose not known to man.

And if we put our trust in Him,

one day we'll understand."

What if you woke up today with only the things you thanked God for yesterday?

Debbie Clews, Barrie, Ontario

A Mother's Prayer of Faith

I was born in New York State but my husband, Christopher, and I now live in Wiarton, Ontario. In 2000, we were enjoying a visit with company outdoors at our home. I had to excuse myself to go to the bathroom in the house. Nobody knew that I had passed out.

My smart cat, Q-tip, sensed that there was something wrong with me. With unusual meows, he went to "tell" my husband about it. Christopher came in and saw me on the floor. I had blood coming out of my nose and mouth. He knew that I had been getting a lot of migraine headaches recently and called 911. They took me to the hospital in Wiarton and then I was moved to Owen Sound. Later I was transferred, by helicopter, to a rehabilitation hospital in London, Ontario.

I had apparently suffered a brain aneurism and doctors did surgery to try to clip a nerve in my brain. Since they couldn't do this, they took a piece of nerve out instead. I was told that most people would have died in these circumstances.

I was unconscious for about 6 weeks. When I came to, my struggles of recovery were many. I had to learn to walk, talk and eat again. Learning to walk again was brutal! My sister, Karen, used to encourage me with the children's story of "The Little Engine That Could". I am now walking well again!

Although there was the danger of total speech loss or permanent speech impairment, I do not have any speech impairment problems. I was also repeatedly checked and tested by doctors and surgeons for memory loss. They said that my recovery was successful and very amazing. This ordeal also positively affected my emotions. I don't cry anymore like I used to.

Most remarkably, I no longer have cancer either. After a check-up, the doctor found that only one lymph node out of twelve had something on it. I had to go through chemotherapy and radiation. Although I lost my hair and my eyelashes, Jesus gave me the strength to go through that. I only got sick once.

Throughout all of this, my mother was praying for me. She also had her church in New York praying for me regularly. I believe, without a doubt, that God answered their prayers and brought me complete healing.

My constant reminder of what I went through is my crooked left baby finger. It never became straight again after the aneurism. However, I am fully able to use both hands, and I walk, talk and eat normally.

These medical issues increased my faith tremendously. I knew that God healed me and he's still healing me today of some anger issues. He is the healer of the body, the mind, and the spirit.

Margaret Reynolds, Wiarton, Ontario

A Victory Won

I am a walking miracle. At the age of 55, I am as full of life as I have ever been. Actually even more so, since the Holy Spirit has put a dance in my feet that wasn't there a few years ago.

At the age of 46, I had an ultrasound which revealed 2 large fibroids in my uterus. They were the size of an 18-week pregnancy. Three years later, they were the size of a 20-week pregnancy and were causing discomfort. I was also having abnormally heavy blood flow with my monthlies. I was considering surgery to have the fibroids removed. However, to make a long story short, I never had that surgery because the Lord intervened and I was given the faith to believe for a miracle.

That in itself was a miracle because, at that time, I was still in a religious system in which people did not believe that divine healing is for today. But the Lord was drawing me out of there, and into a new and exciting life with Him. At the age of 51, I was born again and, about a year later, I received the baptism of the Holy Ghost and the gift of tongues.

The miracle that I was looking for didn't happen the way I expected. But the Lord sustained me. I was never sick, nor did I have any pain or discomfort. It was a healing that I had to contend for.

In April of 2012, I was going through a time of uncertainty. I never knew when I would suddenly have a heavy discharge of blood. I don't know if it was the change of life phase I was going through or if it was connected to the fibroids. I never felt that I was to go for medical help. During this time, I learned to walk and commune more with the Lord. One week in particular stands out.

Friends had been at our home that Sunday and they stayed till late into the night. Even before the last one left, I was aware that something unusual was happening. I sat on the toilet for hours, reading and letting the Lord minister to me. He told me that He would heal me. At 2:45 a.m., the Lord prompted me to speak to Saloma, my sister, and invite her to join me in praise and worship during which the Holy Spirit moved powerfully. At 4:30 in the morning, I felt a release and finally went to bed.

Tuesday afternoon, the blood flow started again. As I was wondering about going to Bible study in the evening, the Lord told me to stay home, so I did. The next morning, I was feeling weak from loss of blood, but the Lord told me He would be my strength as I go to the Father's Heart Healing Centre to minister to people who come in for prayer. A group of prayer warriors gathered around me that evening and we declared that the enemy is under our feet. Although I didn't feel different physically, I felt a freedom in the spirit, and praise and worship issued from me all the way home.

Thursday, Friday and Saturday the Lord was my constant strength and support. I was able to do all the physical labour that needed to be done, but only because I knew He was with me.

Sunday morning, I had a larger discharge of blood again. When I asked the Lord what it means and what I am to do, He said, "Stay home," and "It's nothing to do with defeat but your physical body needs rest." I recognized my heavenly Father's divine love and care for me.

That night, I woke up feeling blood clots threatening to come again. This time, instead of asking Saloma to join me in worship, as I first thought God was asking me to do, He spoke to me saying, "I seldom repeat Myself. This time, jump up and down as if dancing on the enemy's head." Although it seemed absurd and risky to do that, I was glad I didn't have to disturb Saloma again.

In August, I was invited to go on a hike on the Bruce Trail with a group of friends. Was it safe for me to plan to go? Naturally speaking, I knew it made no sense to even think of it because of the risk of heavy blood flow, but I felt the Lord encouraging me to go. I had hoped that my condition on the days prior to the day of the hike would be such that I would have reason to believe it will be okay, but that was not to be.

On the morning of the hike, I communed with the Lord about it. He told me to go and all would be well. When I was hesitant, He said, "Just trust Me." I understood that staying home would only postpone the miracle that He wanted to perform. Therefore, I chose to claim the promise which God spoke to Mary, "The power of the Most High shall overshadow thee." Numerous times that forenoon, and on our way to the trail, I had to resist the enemy who brought thoughts of fear: *What if I have a discharge of blood and there'd be no place to go?* But, by the grace of God, I didn't succumb to the negative thoughts and all went well, just as God had said it would. God is so faithful if we will only trust Him.

I feel a victory was won that day. I never had severe hemorrhaging after that. Several times it appeared as though it might come again, and each time I had to resist the enemy who wanted me to succumb to fear, which would have opened the door for him to bring it on again. I don't know exactly when the last time was, but I believe it has been well over a year now since I last had signs of bleeding. I am still believing for the total disappearance of the hard lump in my abdomen, but I praise the Lord for His goodness. It is not causing any problems and most of the time I forget it's there.

Malinda Bowman, Elmira, Ontario

Healing and Deliverance Ministry

My parents, Olive and Maxwell Whyte, originate from England. In 1936, I was born as their first son and seemed to be a healthy child. However, when I was only fourteen months old, I was smitten with bronchial pneumonia in both lungs and, for seven long weeks, I was wavering between life and death. My parents later told me that they had come up against a situation which was beyond their control. There were no drugs for this illness at that time. Our family doctor was a good friend of the family and he did all he could. He told my parents that it was simply a question of whether I would be strong enough to endure the ravages of the attack long enough for my little body to be able to overcome the germs causing this condition. My mother turned to God, although she thought she really had no right to ask God for His help since her devotion to Him had turned colder over the years. She walked up and down the back yard and prayed to God to spare her baby.

Up in his study, unbeknownst to my mom, my father was also praying, in his own way, to what he referred to, at the time, as his impersonal God. He said that it was almost an insolent command. In His great mercy, God heard my parents' plea and my life was spared. My parents told me that this was a real turning point in their lives. They realized that God had answered their prayer and had performed a miracle for me.

When our family wanted to immigrate to Canada after the Second World War, our family had to pass a medical exam. There were three children in the family by then. All of us passed the medical exam with flying colours—except for me. Although the Lord had saved my life and I enjoyed good health for all practical purposes, I was left with badly scarred lung tissue and this made a frightening noise when the doctor applied his stethoscope. Apparently the doctor looked very serious and said, "I cannot allow this boy to go." My parents argued, and explained, and prayed. Finally, and very grudgingly, the doctor said that if they would get x-rays of my chest, they would examine these before making a final decision.

My parents rushed home and through our family doctor, they arranged to have the x-rays taken. The next day, my father went back to the medical examiners for immigration with the x-ray plates. The doctors peered, hesitated, looked very grave, and then finally and very grudgingly, passed him as C-3. They said that the only reason they were doing this was because my parents had some private money from the sale of their home and so they would be able to pay for my care when I become sick. Neither of my parents expected me to get sick, and I didn't!

Our family doctor was anxious to know the results of the x-ray examination. My mother telephoned him. She was quite annoyed with the doctors for making such a fuss when I was so obviously healthy and full of energy. Our doctor pointed out, however, that from a medical point of view, he had never seen such scarring on the lungs of anyone who was walking around! "Such lungs," he said, "are usually seen on dead bodies!" My mother cried triumphantly, "So you must admit that the health our son, David, enjoys is a miracle?" Our dear Baptist doctor, who did not believe in divine healing, had to say, "Yes." However, he took the opportunity to warn my mother lovingly that she must not expect this good state of affairs to continue. He said that, as I grew older, I would become more and more frail until, at the age of twenty-one, I would probably be a semi-invalid! My parents considered this to be the verdict of man, but they were trusting God to complete the work which He had begun in my body when He saved me from death.

I grew up to be six foot tall, fit and healthy. It was rare for me to be absent from work because of ill health. My mother said our God is faithful when we trust Him fully and I have lived my entire life with this same belief.

I did have some reading difficulties when I was at school, but my parents sought the help of the Lord in this too and He guided and helped us. In my late teens, I became somewhat defiant and did the exact things my parents warned me not to do, just to see what would happen. When sometimes disastrous consequences followed, I would be very surprised and always deeply repented when I realised that I had caused my parents pain and anxiety. My parents prayed me through these difficult years.

My mother thought that I would never get married, although I had many girlfriends. She told me that the Lord had told her that He had a wife picked out for me and that she would love her. I had actually proclaimed that I did not intend to get married because I was well looked after at home and didn't want the responsibility of a wife. But my mother believed God.

I began to declare that I would get married when I'm thirty. Some months before my thirtieth birthday, I began to go out with Gen and my parents thought that their prayers would, once again, be answered. One Sunday night after church, I brought Gen over to our home and announced that we were getting married. Gen and I were married on my thirtieth birthday and my mother did, indeed, love her. Since then we've also raised a family and Gen shares one of her own miracle stories elsewhere in this book. I am now 78 years young and have been happily married for 48 years!

My mother's and father's hunger for God grew after I was miraculously healed as a baby. They later began a healing and deliverance ministry in Toronto, Canada, through which thousands of people were set free. In the seventies, week after week, more and more people were being gloriously delivered from the cruel oppression of Satan by the prayer of faith given in the name of Jesus. My mother and father ministered to both Protestants and Catholics, and Jesus healed and delivered them from the grip of Satan. Many were healed of long-lasting illnesses, or instantly delivered from addictions to drugs and alcohol, severe depression, and even suicidal tendencies.

Dave Whyte, Barrie, Ontario

I Shall Not Die, But Live

Psalm 118:17 says "I shall not die, but live, and declare the works of the Lord."

On November 21, 2010, I was admitted to Georgian Bay General Hospital, in Midland, Ontario, in very serious condition. The doctors and nurses were alarmed by my vital signs and perplexed as to the cause. I thought I was experiencing irritable bowel syndrome but, instead, I was near death from an abscess in my ovary that had swelled to the size of two grapefruits. The condition, called pyometra, is incredibly rare in women and only 0.01% of gynecological patients are diagnosed with it. In my case, it was even more unusual since it affected my ovary rather than the uterus. The nurses and doctors told me how very sick I was and how waiting a few more hours would have been too late for them to try to save me.

My sister swiftly informed my friends at church of my grave condition and they began to pray earnestly for me. The doctors and nurses thought I did not understand how sick I was because I was so calm. They got right in my face and told me slowly and clearly, "You are very sick." I replied that I understood, but I was very calm because I felt the presence of God around me.

I was in great pain, and only semi-conscious, but I kept hearing bits of a song in my mind. I could hear a few notes—a word or two. I knew it was significant, but could not quite put it together. Finally, I was able to get enough of the song to realize what a gift from God it was. It was *Angel of the Lord* and the lyrics go like this:

Surely the Angel of the Lord is around me.

I have no cause to fear, my God will not forsake me.

I am His child now, no enemy can touch me.

I will not die but live to tell what He has done.

God made this segment of the song particularly significant to me in that it begins with my name, "Shirley" (Surely). Because of this song, during the week I spent in ICU, fighting pneumonia and septic shock, and enduring endless rounds of antibiotics, treatments, x-rays, and MRIs, as well as endless pain, I was NOT afraid. I KNEW God was taking care of me and that I would survive. Even when emergency surgery was the only option left, I was not afraid because the Holy Spirit never left me.

As I recovered from the illness, nurses would come to introduce themselves. Then they would take my chart to read it, return to my bedside and stand there staring at me. When I asked one nurse why she was staring, she said, "I've never seen anyone with numbers like these who was alive." I was told much later by my doctor that the condition I had is caused by cancer in over 90% of women who are diagnosed with it, but tests showed no cancer.

Friends, God is real! Believe and be saved.

Shirley Krayden, Port McNicoll, Ontario

Spreading Love in the Streets

I have many stories through which God can be glorified. They began when I was about 25 years old, when I was at a low point in my life. I was fired from my job as a registered nurse and lost my home. Nothing was going my way. I had been with my boyfriend, who was a dentist, for about three years, but he was offering me no support.

I felt like I had always known Jesus because I accepted Him into my heart when I was only five. But I wasn't living for Him. I first found out about the awesome love of Jesus when I cried out to Him at that depressing time and began going to church. I decided I had enough of the lifestyle I had been living. I quit the bar scene and drinking. My addiction to the party scene, including drinking, drugs and men, faded away too.

I've never looked back since that time. Friends had told me that it's just a phase I'm going through and that this infatuation with Jesus would pass. But I denied it and held on to Him. I remembered the scripture in which Jesus said, "If you deny me before men, then I will deny you before my Father in heaven." I couldn't deny the miracles that God had done in my life, like taking away the addictions, meeting my needs, and blessing me in many ways.

I believed in Jesus so much that I wanted others to know Him too. Therefore I began to search for tools that would help me to bring people to Him. I learned some of them from Todd

White, a "street evangelist" whom I met while living in Texas. At a conference where Todd was teaching, each day we would be learning something, and then we would go out into the streets to "try it out". We learned about the power that the love of Jesus has on people. When we would tell complete strangers that Jesus truly loves them, they would often be in tears. When we approached people, I would ask, "Can we pray for you?" and the answer was always, "Yes!" It was such a pleasure to see people soften up to Jesus. We would be bold enough to pray for pain in their body to go away, and more often than not, the pain would lessen or disappear, and they would feel heat or electricity go through their body when we laid hands on them.

My husband and I have been married for ten years now and we have two wonderful boys. This too is somewhat of a miracle. I had decided not to kiss any more men until my wedding day because of my former addiction to men. In college, I even had a "kissing contest" going on with a friend of mine. The challenge was who could kiss the most guys. I think I was up to about 200 when I decided to quit. After reading some books given to me by the pastor's daughter of our church, I wanted to remain pure in heart and mind for my future husband. When I read the first book, *I Kissed Dating Goodbye*, I didn't think that I could do it, or even wanted to do it, because I thought that, at the age of 26, I was running out of time to find a husband, and I couldn't give six months of my life to God. However, after reading the second book, *My Knight in Shining Armour*, I knew that I could remain pure for my "knight". I made a list of everything that I wanted in a man. One of the things I told God is that I don't care what he does for a living or how much money he makes, as long as this man loves God above all things. I gave God six months of my time and attention, focusing my time on Bible studies and church, and I actually stopped looking for a man.

My future husband-to-be started coming to my church (right after I told God I would give Him six months of my time and attention) and, when we first met, he thought I was *not* the one for him. About a year later, he asked me if I wanted to start courting, specifically with the intention of marriage in mind. Five weeks later, we were engaged, and 5 months after that, we were married! During our courtship, we both knew that God had put us together. But we were still looking for a confirmation from God that we were meant to be together forever. This involved a specific "fleece" that my husband-to-be had made with God. We were at a conference in a church in Toronto with thousands of people around us. After three days of not hearing anything from God, and just as we were leaving the conference to head home, a guy approached us and asked me, "Excuse me, but are you engaged?" I replied, "No." Then my husband-to-be received a prophetic word during which the person saw a picture of a peanut butter and jelly sandwich with no crust around it. This was it! This was the confirmation from God!

When this person said he didn't know why there is no crust around the sandwich, my husband-to-be explained: "I'll tell you why… About six months ago, I told God that I needed a code word for my future wife, and that code word was *peanut butter and jelly sandwich with the crust cut off.*" It was so amazing to both of us that this specific word of confirmation was given to us by God through a stranger!

My friend's husband, who was a skeptic when it comes to the power of Jesus, came home while I was visiting her in

Pennsylvania. He was dealing with severe, right-sided abdominal pain, really expecting to need surgery. We laid our hands on his abdomen and I cursed that pain. He and I felt movement and his wife felt heat. The pain left and he was excited. It's been years now and there have been no issues since.

Then, a few months back, I was visiting with them again in Pennsylvania. He allowed me to pray for him again and he felt surgery being done in his brain, as if electricity was connecting things! He was so amazed that he started sharing powerful dreams with us that were very prophetic and supernatural. They were surely from God and I was able to help interpret these dreams for him! His wife is so happy in her marriage now that he is also a believer!

I had a friend named John, whom I hadn't seen in about 15 years. He and his wife, Jane, had never been exposed to "the new me". They also did not really know Jesus. A couple of years ago, when I had a chance to reconnect with John, he was suffering from some back pain. I prayed for his back, and then asked him, "How does that feel?" His reply was, "I don't really know…" Then, placing his hand on his heart, he said, "It feels good right here!" To me, that was a miracle, because I had gone to see him with a mission on my mind—a mission to lead him to Jesus. The best miracle is seeing people have hope again.

The same night that I reconnected with my friends, John and Jane, I also reconnected with my old boyfriend. He asked me why I had become a Christian and why I had changed so much. After I told him that I had tried everything else and nothing was working, he became curious. When I told him how I had remained pure and not kissed my husband until I was married to him, he was shocked and shouted out in awe, "But you were a nymphomaniac!" Then I offered to pray for him because he had been diagnosed with MS. He was twitching a lot before I prayed for him, but the twitching stopped and did not return for the rest of the evening.

During dinner, my friend, John, started to make some unusual and inappropriate comments and became confused. He was even calling his wife, Jane, by a different name. I thought that all ground had been lost and felt very defeated. I wondered whether anything I had said or done in the last few hours had been truly effective. I was quite disappointed and started praying under my breath. All of a sudden John said, "What's happening to me?" and ran into the bathroom attempting to throw up, with only spit and mucous coming out. I instantly realized that he was getting deliverance and I explained to him that the devil is trying to use him to destroy what God is trying to do for him today. Then I showed him some deliverance videos on YouTube and prayed for deliverance for him right then and there. John received a touch from God and returned to normal again! His wife and son also wanted prayer after what they had just witnessed. What a glorious weekend!

I have another friend who called me, about four years ago, to tell me that she had been suffering from severe depression. Her husband had just left her and her doctor wanted to put her on medication. It was a defining moment in her life. She was particularly sad because she had always wanted children, despite the fact that doctors had told her that she would never be able to have them. She was diagnosed as being "post-menopausal" at the very young age of 22.

During her 2-year marriage, she had never used protection because, according to doctors, there could be no possibility of pregnancy. I received a free flight to Arizona, a free car, and a beautiful, free home so that I could spend ten days with my friend. Thank you, Jesus, for the provision! I prayed with her, worshiped in her home, and helped her in any way I could. I told her about the Word of the Lord—about His desire for her to bear children. I broke the curse spoken by medical professionals and rebuked Satan from her life. Then I boldly laid hands on her belly and prayed, "In the name of Jesus, you will conceive and you will have a baby," She later called me to tell me that she was seven weeks pregnant. It was seven weeks exactly to the day of the prayer! My friend now has a beautiful, precious, three-year-old girl. Since this time, there have been four other women who had difficulty conceiving and whom I prayed for. They all became pregnant too.

People began to question me about my faith and my decision for Christ. I had to stand up for my beliefs. The Lord showed me how much He loves them and I told them so. When I began to talk about the realm of the supernatural, they told me about some rather strange and evil spiritual things that had been happening to them. They seemed to be tormented in their own bedrooms by evil spirits. Since they have accepted Jesus, the torments have stopped. When I was with them, their friends would join in and pray with us and, as a result, some of their friends have become saved too and have experienced the supernatural. We kind of have church wherever we go.

Someone close to me had an encounter with the Lord while I was in the room with her at a young age. She had been addicted to speed and had difficulties coping. Although she did not really know how to pray, one night, she asked God to give her peace and she experienced Him in a supernatural way as she saw a window opening and closing. She yelled out, "I want the light. I want the light!" Then she heard a voice tell her, "Do not be afraid!" At that moment, a dark figure fled out of her room and God told her that He was healing her spiritual eyes and ears (because she had no physical problems at the time). During the following year, she experienced intense dreams and visions. She also saw a ball of fire go into her body from the ceiling and she felt electricity travel up and down her spine. In an audible voice, she heard God tell her that she was not to go to an occult fair the next day, and that she would meet someone who would teach her about God.

This woman also smoked 2 packs of cigarettes a day. After meeting her spiritual Father, He told her that smoking was a demon and that she should pray against the spirit. When she did, she instantly quit smoking. She later wanted to be able to speak in tongues (as taught in the Bible) but she couldn't do it. However, after deliverance, she finally did receive the gift of tongues from the Lord. It is an amazing feeling to know that I was a part of this experience and it saved my life as well as hers!

I had been trying to befriend our neighbours for a number of months. A few weeks ago, I went over to their place and shared with them about the movie called "Holy Ghost". It features the rock group Korn, and I asked them if they were familiar with that band. They replied that it's their favourite group and were surprised to hear that the former bass player is now a Christian. Apparently, the media didn't tell that side of the story. It was exactly what they needed to hear to open their hearts to the Lord. I ended up talking with them about God for hours that day.

I also shared with them about how Todd White often has a "word of knowledge" from God that helps people to trust in Him. I gave the example of having a word of knowledge about a person who had pain in their left knee and when Todd prayed against that pain, it would go away. I was totally unaware that my neighbour had a knee problem at the time—in her left knee! As she lifted up her skirt so I could see her left knee with a tensor bandage on it, she said, "Well, I guess you can pray for *me* then." It was as if God had given me a word of knowledge for her too. I encouraged her husband to touch her knee for her healing while I prayed, in order to show them that the power doesn't come from me, but from Jesus. The pain left and she removed the tensor bandage on her own! I blessed the young couple and told them about the love of Jesus and that there is no condemnation in Christ Jesus. This touched her husband and he, an atheist, even prayed with me for himself, although he feared that he had lived a terrible life and could not be forgiven for the "unforgivable sin" of unbelief. When I told him that this is a lie from the devil, and that God loves him and has a purpose for his life, he looked me in the eyes in awe and simply said, "That felt amazing!" He had felt a tangible heat and touch from the supernatural realm of Jesus. He shared that he had lived in orphanages as a child, lost a child of his own, and had experienced other life challenges that had made him very angry, but this day had given him hope.

Our church has a little "street team" that goes out. There are usually about five to eight of us and we go out rain or shine. We meet people in the streets and tell them about the love of Jesus and, with respect, offer to pray for them. Many respond with questions and tears. We also go into some of the businesses in town and bless them. One day, we went out earlier than normal and God arranged for us to meet up with a friend. We asked if we could pray for her. She wanted prayer for someone in her family, whom I happened to know. Later, when I got home, I texted my friend to ask if she felt our prayer and this was her response: *"Oh my goodness, Anne-Marie, thank you!!!!!! I knew someone was praying because today I had horrible anxiety and felt like I'd never enjoy life. Did not feel like myself at all. And tonight the anxiety lifted 90% and the feeling of despair and hopelessness is gone. Your prayers are making a difference out there. Xoxo. Love you. I could cry. God is so good, so faithful, never leaving us alone and always showing up. xo."*

One day, I met a music producer and three band members at the beach where I take my kids swimming. They were drinking beer while driving their Sea-Doos, which is dangerous and illegal. I was going to approach them about it, but then God intervened instead. Two other green Sea-Doos appeared. Thinking that these were police Sea-Doos, the men became agitated and instantly dumped out their beers. I thought, *"Wow God, you got them to do what I wanted them to do...that fast!"* I was pleased, but I felt like the Lord wanted to do more. As I heard the young tattooed men singing and talking about bands, I walked over to them and began to ask them about their band. They introduced the music producer and themselves and told me that they had just played a concert on an island. I told them that I don't really know much about secular or the world's music because I only listen to Christian music. When I suggested they connect with a local Christian station, they looked at me as if I were crazy. Then I said, "I really just came over to pray for you guys." I asked them if that would be OK, and they replied, "Yeah!" I prayed a prophetic prayer over two of the guys about the destiny of their lives, and for their music to bless people and bring healing and revelation to people. I was decreeing what the Lord truly wants them to do with their music, and I blessed them. They loved it and were blown away! They had never received prayer like this before. One of them believed in God and he showed me his tattoos, including tattoos of a cross, Jesus, and Mary. They thanked me for the prayers and asked me to pray for their music producer too. At this point, the producer brought out a white capsule, opened it up, and sniffed it while I prayed. He was trying to test me, but I continued my prayer, adding that there's no high like the Most High and that Jesus loves him. Afterwards, he hugged me and said that this was very touching.

Recently, I took a homeless girl to church with me and dropped her off at her hotel room afterwards. When she invited me in, there were all kinds of people there doing drugs at 1:00 o'clock in the afternoon. At first I was in shock, but then I simply said loudly, "Jesus loves you guys!" One of the guys was on the bed, making out with his girlfriend. He looked at me with the most evil eyes and said, "What?" Then I left. I didn't know whether to go to the cops to report them, or whether to go back to my church to pray for them. I decided to go back to the church for our usual afterglow gathering, when people stay after the service to receive prayer and enjoy fellowship. About ten of us prayed heavily for this group of young people.

When another of my friends and I left the church, we drove by that hotel again and found two of the guys hanging out in the parking lot. They were scary and intimidating. We became friendly with them and then asked if we could pray for one of them and his girlfriend. As we laid hands on him, tears started to pour out. He had been in jail and now he was being touched by the presence of God. It was really overwhelming him. He said that he didn't know what it was, but something was happening to him. It was intense and amazing to see Jesus instantly change them from being high on something to being high on Jesus! The toughest guy was in tears and didn't know that when God comes on the scene, people usually cry. God was using me to reach these guys for Jesus.

My formerly homeless friend also found a new life. She found a native man who truly cares for her and he, too, has become saved by the love of God.

If we want to see God move, we have to take a risk and become involved with people; we have to step out of our comfort zone and practice talking about Him with others. Last Halloween, a few friends and I went to a "witch walk". There were hundreds of people. I wrote "Free Spiritual Readings" on a big piece of construction paper. People were curious about it and came to us. We ended up praying for about 20 people and it was a powerful time with God where some also invited Jesus into their hearts!

I used to live on an Indian reserve, where I worked as a registered nurse. God gave me a heart for our Canadian native people. I feel He wants me to show them the truth in order to be set free. I recently found out that I had a great-great-grandfather who owned a store on a native reserve, near where I currently reside. God has a plan and I sense that He will open doors for me to minister in this area to the native people, including my long lost relatives!

Last year, I met a native woman at a daycare place. She knew that I was Christian and asked me not to talk about Jesus because she had her own native beliefs. I agreed, but she kept bringing up the subject about Jesus and saw the love of God in me. On several occasions, over a period of about a year, when God put it on my heart, I would go to her house to visit her. She usually had a number of friends there who would be drinking and doing drugs outside. She allowed me to pray for her over and over again, and she began to see the power of God. When she had these gatherings, I was able to preach to all of her friends. They were mostly against going to church, but they listened to me. They allowed me to pray for them and they felt God's presence right where they were. I also sometimes had touching words of knowledge for them. Little by little, the walls came down and they would be in tears. They'd run into me at times and would remember me, although I had forgotten their names. I believe that it was Jesus they were really remembering.

My friend had lost her partner, the father of her child, at the young age of 33 due to a blood clot. She was lost spiritually and had no desire to go on living. She felt that nobody loved her. Then I told her that Jesus loves her and she instantly changed. It was like a new person had been born. It was an intense and overwhelming change. She began to recognize the power within herself and proclaimed the love of Jesus to others too. There had been some demonic activity in her life and her home (banging on the walls, blankets being ripped off her children, electronics going on and off), but it all suddenly stopped after she finally got so annoyed with it that she couldn't sleep and yelled, "if you don't stop, I'll call Anne-Marie and she will come!!!" The activity stopped. The demon knew that I represented Jesus. This woman also told me that, one day, a Bible appeared in her home out of nowhere. This, of course, helped her grow in her knowledge of the Lord. Her kids also love having her read it to them every night.

Her brother had told her that he doesn't just think Jesus is real, but he *knows* Jesus is real. When he was only 12, he was about to commit suicide. He asked Jesus to prove that He is real and Jesus just showed up in his room! It scared him so much that he ran right through him. They celebrated that he made it to his 30th birthday and he is fine now. He is enjoying his family too.

Another friend of mine is a religion teacher in a Catholic high school. Reconnecting with her on a deeper level, after many years, included sharing what Jesus has done in my life. This led her to have her own experiences with God. One day, as I was making us lunch, I was casually telling her stories of how Jesus has done great things through my many experiences. I had my back to her and she asked me to give her a hug because she was crying. As I did, she said, "I think Jesus is using you to help me!" She now talks about the deeper things of Jesus. Even her kids are excited about Jesus and her mother-in-law shares only things about Jesus on Facebook now. She is also having a very positive effect on her students and is helping them strengthen their relationship with Christ. The Christian radio station in our area has also been a blessing to her and she was led to begin to go to church again. Her husband then also wanted to attend church! We often meet and have wonderful times with the Lord, which is keeping her fed for her ministry as a religion teacher until they find the right church for their family.

A friend of mine has also experienced some amazing things of God. I hadn't seen her in a number of years. When we got together, she began to tell me that her son is going through a hard time at his school. I offered to pray for my friend and her family, and was led by the Holy Spirit to pray at a deeper spiritual level than what she may have been used to hearing. She doubted that she could have a relationship with God like I have. When I told her that she needed an experience with God, and prayed for her to have such an experience, she literally did! A week or so later, she woke up in the middle of the night, after having some kind of demonic attack preventing her from breathing properly. She couldn't find the yoga book that she was looking for, so she reached for her Bible and began to cry out to God. She was instantly set free of whatever it was that was tormenting her that night.

Now she is very outgoing and prays for her family and others in times of need. Recently, her young son was outdoors and was attacked by mosquitos. He was literally covered in huge, infected blotches all over his back and body. There was no medication available, so she thought "*I'll just do what my friend, Anne-Marie, does.*" She prayed for healing for her son and believed it would come. He did not have to suffer any terrible itching. Later that night, the huge, red blotches had almost completely disappeared and there were photos to prove it. This had a positive effect on the family in the area of faith and she now prays regularly with me for others.

A short time ago, her aunt called and asked my friend and me to pray for her before undergoing some tests for cancer, even though her husband is a well-known doctor. We prayed for her and it turned out that everything was fine. No cancer was found! We encouraged her to continue to talk to Jesus.

This contagious effect of seeing amazing miracles through the power of prayer with friends, and friends of friends, and even strangers continues day by day. On my recent trip to the USA, one girl got deliverance, others fell down under the power of the Holy Spirit, and still others almost fell down or were swayed by the Spirit of God. Some cried heavily, others gently, and some rested in the simple encouragement that Jesus loves them. These are all tangible experiences with our heavenly Father! I am so thankful for open hearts and I love that others are joining me in prayer, because when we pray together, we stay together. My dream is that the next generation will go into the streets and go beyond what we are seeing and doing—all through prayer with the love of Jesus.

Anne-Marie, Barrie, Ontario

My Story for God's Glory

I have to thank God for so many wonderful things that have happened to me. I am writing this personal testimony letter to my family, friends and anyone else who wants to know more about our loving God and what He has done in my life. As Christians, we are encouraged to give testimonies to strengthen our own faith and to encourage one another. God often uses the experiences of ordinary people to teach others.

I've been interested in supernatural or divine healing for many years because of a personal experience that I had well before I understood any of it. In order to give a complete testimony about this experience, I would have to go back to the time of my birth. So here's my story:

I was born in Essen, Germany, on October 9, 1957 with a dislocated right hip that went undetected at birth. My mother noticed very early in my childhood that, when I was learning to walk, I was already limping. She pointed this out to our family pediatrician, but was told that the uneven walk was because I was chubby and that I would grow out of it.

As a young child, I must have had some discomfort in that hip fairly often because I remember that I did not often run when playing, and I always wanted to find a place to sit down

194

when my mother took me shopping with her, or when we went on a Sunday family outing that included walking.

My mother was persistent with the doctor, telling him that she thought there was something wrong with the hip. Finally, when I was 7 years old, I underwent x-rays which indicated that the bone was not properly positioned in the hip socket, which caused the discomfort and the limp. Corrective surgery was scheduled and I spent a considerable amount of time in a hospital with a cast around my waist and abdomen, reaching down to the bottom of my right leg. The Frankenstein-style stitches that the surgeons did in those days are still a visible sign of that childhood surgery.

While in the hospital in Germany, in the early 60s, my parents were not allowed to visit me at my bedside. My mother visited, but was only permitted to see me through a large glass window located at the front of the room that I was in. She decided to communicate with me using a hard cover notebook, in which she would write letters to me, telling me about what the family was up to, about how much she loved me, and how she wished she could be with me. Even at this very young age, I liked writing back to her in this letter format. As a matter of fact, letter writing would eventually become an important part of my life in many ways. Since I was quite young, I was probably not able to read my mom's letters all by myself. Sometimes the nurses read those kind words to me. These letters of love from my mother were the first words of healing for me.

My family immigrated to Canada in the summer of 1967. During my elementary school years, like most kids, I walked to school, played, skipped, played badminton, rode a bike and swam often. However, I was never very active in sports, especially sports that involved running. I always limped because one of my legs was shorter than the other. During the years after my first surgery, I had to wear orthopaedic shoes—the laced, boot-like type of shoe with one sole much higher than the other. I eventually became frustrated with these boots and, like many stubborn, young children, I refused to wear them anymore, despite what the doctor and my parents said.

During my teens, I was still not very active. The only school sport I liked was volleyball (it didn't involve much running). However, I did learn how to ski in high school and, despite the fact that one leg was shorter than the other and I never became an expert at it, I was usually able to keep up with my friends.

As a young teen, I was fortunate to participate in several school trips that took me away from home for weeks at a time. I spent several weeks in England and almost a whole summer in Quebec. During these lengthy absences from home, I developed a love for writing letters. I remember that my letters to home were always very lengthy and quite detailed, with reports on where I had been, what I had seen, and especially what I felt about my experiences away from home. Not only did I write home often, but I also wrote regularly to several of my friends. Just as much as writing them, I loved receiving letters from my family and friends.

For our first few years in Canada, we lived in Windsor, Ontario, and then we moved to Kingsville, where I attended high school. Although my parents never prayed at home or took us to church, I was always seeking to know and understand God. Yet He seemed so far away. Thanks to an invitation from one of my close friends, I agreed to attend a youth retreat weekend called "COR" during one of my senior years in high school. This, I believe, was the beginning of my efforts in discovering and developing my faith. It was a chance to learn about who we are—particularly who we are in our family, and in the big family of God. I remember that one of the exercises we were asked to do was to write a letter to our mother and our father, expressing our hidden feelings to them. Little did we know that our parents had also been asked to write us letters— letters of love, letters of forgiveness, letters of healing! These letters were very precious to us because many of us, as teens, tended to get the impression that no one cares about us and no one understands us—not even our parents. I was very emotional while reading those letters of healing!

During my final year of high school, I was asked to write a very special goodbye letter on behalf of my graduating class. Writing this valedictorian address for the evening of our high school graduation ceremonies was a challenge for me, but it was also a pleasure. One very important statement that I made in that letter had actually come from my mother. She had often said to me, "What you have learned can never be taken away from you. It will be with you forever!" Of course, like most teens, at 18, I thought I had all the knowledge I will ever need! At that time, I barely realized how true those words from my mom actually were. I would later learn that the Bible teaches us that "people are destroyed from lack of knowledge." (Hosea 4:6, NIV) The unshakable knowledge that I have now, at 57, is that Jesus loves me—enough to die for me—enough to allow Himself to be beaten and put to death in order to take the punishment for *my* sins! If only I had possessed *that* knowledge when I was 18 and just starting out into this crazy, pain-filled world.

I was learning that God wants us all to have knowledge of Him. Isaiah, one of the prophets of the Old Testament, was sent by God to tell the world that, in the end, "the earth will be filled with the knowledge of the Lord." (Isaiah 11:9, NIV) Over the last couple of decades, I've come to realize that God gives us so much during our lifetime here on earth, but the most important thing He gives us is knowledge and wisdom to take into eternity with us. All of our physical "stuff" stays here, no matter how much or how little we have when we die. Having lost and wasted much over the years, I've learned that my mother was definitely right: Only knowledge can never be taken away from you!

During my years at the University of Western Ontario in London, I also remember writing many letters to family members, friends who were attending other universities, and friends who were still living in our home town. Writing letters seemed to be my way of filling some not-so-busy hours and of recording my experiences and feelings.

The third year of my university studies was spent in France. During the year that I spent studying at the Université de Besançon, I wrote home often and, when I returned home to my parent's place after that lengthy absence, my mother presented me with the collection of my letters, all bound together in a small, yellow binder. Because I had written almost daily about my experiences and my trips to other countries in Europe, the collection of letters really resembled a journal, which I kept as a memento of that year. I was just as fond of all the letters that I had received from family and friends over the years, and I kept those in a keepsake box.

While I was in Europe, I attended church regularly and visited several well-known cathedrals. I admired them, and took in the vastness of the buildings and the beautiful stained glass windows. I even prayed in the pews. However, I never sensed the presence of God or Jesus, and didn't even know the Holy Spirit.

After I finished university, I moved even farther away from home to Scarborough, Ontario. Since I did not know anyone there, and since I had previous experience in folk dance and enjoyed it very much, I decided to join a Toronto ethnic folk dance group and later helped to found a brand new folk dance group at a German club in Brampton. Dancing kept me busy and allowed me to meet many people who became very dear to me. I was a member of this newer folk dance group for many years but eventually I was forced to slow down, and sometimes even sit out of practices or performances, because my right hip was often sore when dancing.

I was married in 1991 and soon afterwards my husband and I had our son, Johnathan James, our pride and joy. We moved away from the big city to Angus, Ontario, and were therefore too far away from the dance group to be able to continue to dance with them. I probably wouldn't have been very useful to the group anyways because, by this time, I was already in pain quite often. I began to take anti-inflammatory medication to deal with the pain, but it continued to get worse year after year. By the time my son was a toddler, I was barely able to keep up with him when he ran, because my hip was always too sore to be able to chase him—even for fun! It was also difficult to lift him up since this put too much stress on my right hip. The hip joint would "slip out" with an extreme shot of pain very regularly. Eventually, I was not able to walk past our neighbour's house to my son's school bus stop anymore, and I often had to crawl up the stairs to bed at night due to the severe pain.

The medication was not helping and my family physician could not do anything else for me. I requested to be referred to a specialist to check out what could be done. After being referred to a local specialist in Barrie, who was also unable to do anything for me, I was sent to be examined by a top orthopaedic surgeon at Sunnybrook Hospital in Toronto. The x-rays showed that my hip bone was not correctly positioned in the hip socket and that there was insufficient space between the pelvic bone and the femur bone—they were rubbing together and causing extreme pain with every step. Surgery was scheduled, along with a one-week stay at a rehabilitation hospital to help with my recovery after the surgery.

This was in 1997. I was 39 years old and my son was in Kindergarten when the surgery was performed at Sunnybrook. At the hands of the chief surgeon, Dr. Joseph Schatzker, and with the help of God, the surgery was a huge success. Although I had many months of physical healing ahead of me, I progressed better than expected and eventually regained complete mobility.

During my time at St. John's Rehabilitation Hospital, I had one of the most unusual experiences of my life up to that point. I literally saw Jesus! Shortly after being admitted to the rehabilitation hospital, one of the nurses told my roommate and me that a "healing service" was going to take place in the hospital chapel the next day. I did not really know what to expect, but I was a believer and I thought I should attend. After all, I was at this hospital for "healing".

I needed a lot of healing though. Not only physical healing for my hip, but healing in every sense of the word! I needed *physical healing* for pain. I needed *spiritual healing* to help me believe and trust more in God. I needed *financial healing* because we were broke. As a matter of fact, we had just declared bankruptcy the previous year—that was something that I thought I would never in a million years have to go through. I was also unemployed at the time because I was supposed to be healing for several months. In addition, I needed *emotional healing*. By this, I mean to say that my mood was very sombre at the time. I had been depressed about all the things that were not going right in my life, and about all the things I couldn't do at the time—which included playing with my son, whom I missed a lot while I was in the hospital. I also desperately needed *relationship healing*. Without going into the details, my relationship with my husband was not ideal at the time. Our lack of communication, and the stress in our work and home life were to blame. As a matter of fact, the last words I heard from my husband over the telephone in the hospital the previous day were words of anger. I was so depressed, shaken, broken, and confused that I believed, in his anger, he had taken my 5-year old son, grabbed his passport, and taken him out of the country without my knowledge. These thoughts tormented me all day and all night because I was not getting any answer when I attempted to call them at home.

In this utterly depressed and broken state, I was wheeled into the chapel in a wheelchair, just before the healing service was to begin. I felt like I was in the worst state I had ever experienced in my life. It was the worst day of my life up to that day and I don't think I've had a worse day since. I felt like I was in the deepest pit and there was no way out. I was stuck in a hospital with ALL kinds of PAIN, crying through the night.

Although my eyes were dry when the music began and two guest singers began to sing hymns, it was not long before I began to weep uncontrollably. The service had not even really begun yet when I very clearly saw my Lord, Jesus, standing at the front of the chapel. It was a beautiful vision that I had never experienced before! I melted with humility…I realized, at that moment, that Jesus is always with us—even at the very worst moments in our life—to help us with our physical pain, spiritual pain, financial pain, emotional pain, and relationship pain.

Because I was crying and could not stop, a nurse came to me to ask me what was wrong. She asked if I was in too much pain and if I wanted to be taken back to my room. I told her that I was fine. At last, I really was fine, realizing that Jesus is real and knowing that He is with me—no matter what! "He will not leave us or forsake us," is a verse that I later read in the Bible. God had planned this moment. He brought me to the right place, at the right time, to learn this one truth!

Literally seeing Jesus is not a common thing, and I kept this experience totally to myself for fear of being laughed at if I told the story to anyone. Like many people, I was never able to talk to anyone about God, Jesus, or religion in general. This was a very personal and private subject for me.

Although I attended Sunday services regularly with my son, I was never able to connect at church. I felt alone and was not able to share with other members, or join a group that might have been able to help me draw closer to God. My husband and my extended family were no source of help either. As far as I could discern, they were not interested in church or in God. I never talked about my faith with anyone, except when reading Bible stories to my young son, who, due to his tender age, was not able to offer any feedback or comments at the time.

As a result of my encounter with the living Jesus, during the early months of my recovery at home, I began to want to know Him more intimately. However, this was difficult for me since I was so alone in my quest. For the first time in my life, I decided to begin to read the Bible to try to learn more about God and Jesus. Although I had attended a traditional church almost all of my life, I had never heard that we should all read the Bible and become familiar with the Word of God ourselves. The big Bible I had at the time had been given to my mother by the church on the occasion of my father's death. She later passed it on to me and I had told myself that I would read it "one of these days". However, despite my studies in several languages, I found it difficult to concentrate on the meanings, and I have to admit that it was hard to understand. I made some headway reading a small portion of it while I was still laid up in bed most of the day, during my recovery from surgery. I slowly progressed from bed rest to crutches, and then to a walker. As soon as I was up and about more, the Bible reading fell by the wayside.

I was still off work but wanted to do some home studies in entrepreneurship since I hoped to start a home-based business after my recovery. My studies centered on improving my computer skills with various programs and my overall business skills. As an experienced translator, my main business idea was to develop a translation business, based in my home. To complement that income, in case I did not receive enough translation contracts during the starting phase of the business, I decided to take a correspondence course in Medical Transcription (not translation but transcription). Besides languages, I had been interested in human biology during my university years and the human biology aspect of this medical transcription course intrigued me. I enjoyed learning about the human body and many of the problems, illnesses, and diseases that humans suffer with. Little did I know that God had a plan for this knowledge. He was leading me into a field that I eventually became fascinated with: Divine healing of body, mind and spirit!

After finishing some adult education courses in 1998, less than one year after my hip surgery, I started my business. God blessed me in this business venture right from day one. The one and only existing translation business in this area, which happened to be based in Barrie, and which I thought would be my number one competition, turned out to be my number one provider of work right from the start! Coincidence? I think not! God had this plan all worked out before I even started my business. I really was "blessed" during my first 5 years of self-employment for I was always busy, and never once had to seek out a customer or advertise in any way. They just came to me through word of mouth. I never had to rely on my "backup" source of income (medical transcription) at all. My translation business was all I needed to provide the income we required.

Being able to work from home was a blessing in several ways. I was able to have flexible work hours and was almost always available for my son when he came home from school at

4:00 p.m. The days were usually busy but I also had some tasks to accomplish that did not require my full attention. During the hours that I did invoicing, record keeping, bill payments and filing, I started to tune in to television programs that interested me. At first these were stories such as "North of Sixty"—a drama series about a Métis community in Northern Canada and their daily struggles. Later I started to listen to talk shows which also focused on people's daily struggles. More often than not, these included struggles with alcohol, drugs, divorce, abuse, loneliness, illness, depression, identity issues, and so many of the other ills that we tend to struggle with.

After a period of time, I became very tired of hearing so many stories about stress and anxiety in people's lives. It was really getting to me to hear that so many individuals struggle so much, and so few actually find help and hope for their problems. I longed to hear some good news in real people's lives. God knew exactly what I needed and how to help me! He led me to start tuning in to totally different programs. In about 2003, I started to watch programs that I still watch today because they were, and still are, so uplifting. **They made me see and believe that good things are still happening daily in the world and that these good things were all due to a firm belief people had in God the Father, Jesus the Son, and the Holy Spirit.**

Some of the programs that I still listen to regularly include "Enjoying Everyday Life" with Joyce Meyers, "Quick Study" with Rod and Janice Hembree, "Life Today" with James and Betty Robison, "It's a New Day" with Willard and Betty Thiessen, and Bob and Audrey Meisner, "This is Your Day" with Benny Hinn, "The Gospel Truth" with Andrew Wommack, and "It's Supernatural" with Sid Roth.

At the end of 2004, I got to know Anna and Lewis Sabo. I had known them before this through our children's school and our church, but only as acquaintances. Through a business relationship, I became friends with Lewis and would travel to various business functions with him, and occasionally with his wife, Anna. On many occasions, we would talk about the great things God can do, and is doing in our life, or the life of a loved one. Several of our talks centered on healing, and included accounts of personal experiences with divine healing. Over the next months, Anna and Lewis became very good friends to me—friends that I trusted to talk to about my faith issues and religion. The business relationship I had with them was fading while a precious friendship was developing. I now know that God had all this planned in advance. He put these two loving people into my life to be prayerful, helpful, trustworthy friends—just what I needed most at that point in my life.

I used to get very emotional watching healing services, such as the miracle crusades that Benny Hinn hosted all over the world. Over and over again, I would cry, standing in front of the television set, as I watched people instantly receive physical healing. When young children who were lame or disabled walked or ran across the stage, my heart rejoiced for them. I would remember all the pain that I had suffered as a child and as an adult.

Many of the television programs that I was watching, or often just listening to, taught about "a personal relationship with Jesus Christ". I used to wonder how on earth anyone could have "a relationship" with God. After hearing many people tell their personal stories about how it happened to them, and how their lives had been completely changed through their relationship with Jesus, I developed a deep desire to have that too. I longed to have what these happy people on TV had. I also wanted everyone in my family and extended family to have this happiness and joy that everyone was talking about.

Like me, my mother had suffered with pain in her body for many years. I longed to see her at one of these healing events and to see God heal her too. One day, I heard on TV that Benny Hinn would be hosting a miracle healing crusade in Detroit, Michigan. Since my mother and all my siblings live very close to the Detroit border, I decided to ask my mother if she would like to go to that upcoming healing service. I truly did not think she would want to go because she had never shown any interest in church or the things of God while we were growing up. I was completely stunned when she accepted the invitation. I was even more surprised when two of my sisters offered to drive us to Detroit and back, since I did not want to drive in the US. They were not interested in attending the miracle services, but were more than willing to drive and be a part of this quest for healing for our mother.

The day of the healing crusade came. I was praying for my mother's healing. Little did I know that this really was *my day*, not my mom's day. Mom felt very uncomfortable in the tight seats, way up high in the arena, where thousands of people were gathered for hours. Unfortunately her pain did not leave her body that day. However, the worship with thousands of other voices, the message of the gospel, and several testimony stories made me want to accept Jesus as my Lord and Saviour. Along with hundreds of others, I surrendered my heart and my life to

Him that day, in the summer of 2005, and I've never been the same since. I received a new life through Christ. Once again, God knew exactly what He was doing. He brought me to the right place, at the right time, for the right reason—to receive salvation!

On my way home to Angus that Sunday, I couldn't stop thinking about all that had happened at the miracle service and my new relationship with Jesus. I prayed more than I had ever prayed before during that five-hour trip home. I continuously played the only Christian CD that I had in the car—an old Elvis gospel collection that I had never listened to before. To be honest, I don't even know how it got into my car music collection. I suddenly understood and loved the words to every Christian song on that CD and sang them over and over again. One song that I couldn't stop listening to was *He Touched Me!* Little did I know how many more times God would "touch me" over the coming years.

Near the end of 2005, I was invited by my friends, Anna and Lewis, to attend another church in Oro, Ontario. I was very resistant to leaving my traditional church in my home town of Angus. However, after some discussion, I agreed to visit at least once. I was overjoyed with the friendly reception, the people I met, and the inspiring teaching and discussions focussing on having a relationship with Jesus Christ. It was exactly what I needed! God began to work in my life and in my spirit at the Alpha course hosted by my new church. I learned more in the 10 meetings at Alpha than I had in 40 years at the traditional churches I had attended.

I became increasingly interested in reading the Bible and in learning more about salvation and healing. A woman in this Oro church was leading a Bible study and I joined in, continuing my attendance for many years. With the guidance and prayers of this group of women, I grew in my faith. I also really enjoyed being a part of a small group which developed out of my Alpha group. Many amazing, solid Christian friendships formed from these two groups. As during earlier years in my life, I turned again to letter writing in order to share the Good News with every member of my family and extended family. Unfortunately, they were not ready to respond at the time, but several have come to develop a relationship with Jesus since then.

The chief orthopaedic surgeon that God had provided for me did an amazing job of repositioning the bones in my hip to allow me to walk better again. However, after the surgery, I still had residual pain almost every day, especially early in the morning. I also still walked with a limp because my right leg was at least 2.5 cm (about one inch) shorter than the other. Due to the misalignment in my hip, my right foot was always pointing out. My footprints were never straight and this made it challenging to keep my skis parallel when downhill skiing.

Healing Prayer

I still wouldn't be completely pain-free today if God hadn't sent me my best friend, Anna, who gave me a book on prayer for healing. I began to read *How to Heal the Sick,* by Charles and Francis Hunter. One night, in a semi-wakeful moment, I had a vision. The voice in the vision prompted me to pray for healing for a mutual friend of ours. I was actually seeing myself do this, but I fought that prompt vehemently with statements like, "God, I can't do that!" Three times, I heard God's voice say, "Try it!" After my last "I can't," I heard a slightly firmer and louder voice say, "Just do it!"

The remainder of the night was restless and I was unable to sleep. I knew that I couldn't ignore this prompt and that I had to do something. The next morning, I called the two friends who were in my vision, Anna and Joanne, and told them what I had seen and heard. They both responded with enthusiasm to the invitation to pray together. We agreed to meet to pray for Joanne, for the healing of carpal tunnel syndrome, as the vision had prompted. I did this out of obedience to God, although I knew very little about divine healing at the time.

When the time came, I was very nervous and even afraid to begin the prayer for healing because I had never done this before. As a matter of fact, I had never even prayed anything out loud before! Fortunately, I didn't even have to open my mouth. To my great relief, God led my good friend, Anna, who had some experience with healing prayer, to take over. Her prayers flowed and I just stood in silent agreement with her.

During the prayer for the healing of Joanne's wrists, the mention of "hip alignment" came up. Obviously, my friend's hips were not the problem. *How could hips have anything to do with wrists?* I thought. *But maybe that prayer could apply to me, since I was the one still suffering with hip pain and misalignment issues.* When we were finished praying, I mentioned this thought to my friends. Anna quickly replied, "OK, then let's pray for you too!" My friends began to pray for my hip alignment, the lengthening of my shorter leg, and for all pain to leave my body. This was totally unplanned and unexpected, and I did not ask for it—but God planned it all along.

The next day, I noticed that I was standing straight while doing the dishes and that I had no pain all day. I stood in grocery store lines that week and noticed it too. I also noticed that my foot was no longer pointing out on an angle, and that my right leg had grown out to be almost equal length to my left. **I realized that God had given me a miracle!** He had called me in the night so that I would give (prayers), and in the midst of giving, He allowed me to receive (a miracle). When I shared this with my two friends a few days later, they rejoiced with me and we praised God together.

I received my full healing that day, in the spring of 2006, and I haven't had a single right hip pain in over eight years! I praise and glorify God for this continually, for this was one of the plans He had for me all along. His timing is always perfect.

When I was finally healed of long-term pain in my right hip, I could hardly wait to go tell my mother about it. She knew about my pain before anyone else did. She saw it first, as the mother of a toddler who limped. My mother had cried for me as she saw me isolated behind a window in the children's ward of a hospital, unable to go in to comfort her young child of seven who was in pain after hip surgery. She often told me that she wished she was the one with the pain, instead of me. I know that she saw and felt my pain when I was young, and had often wondered why it had to be me.

At the age of 48, when I was fully healed after receiving prayer, I travelled to tell my mother what I had discovered— why I think I was born with this disability and why I had to suffer with pain for so long. I told her I had learned that God allowed this in my life so that, one day, I could give Him all the glory for healing it completely. That "one day" had come! This is one of the plans God has for our life—to give Him glory and honour for what He has done for us. Although I lived with a lot of pain throughout my childhood and adult life, I can now run, hike, dance, swim, bike and even downhill ski pain-free. I can sing **"I Am Free"** and mean it!

My healing journey did not end there! I have had several other wonderful experiences of God's presence and healing touch. My desire to learn more about the way God heals grew and I sought out Scriptures in the Bible relating to healing. I also read many books on the subject, took some training courses in healing ministry, and attended seminars and conferences led by ministers who had the gift of healing. Almost each time, I would hear teaching on the Scripture that says *all* believers can heal the sick (Mark 16:17-18, NLT).

I also heard and read a lot about the baptism with the Holy Spirit, and I began to inquire about how to receive it. Although I received word from one pastor that this baptism wasn't necessary, another pastor was of the opposite opinion. He told me more about it and invited me to receive this special baptism that very weekend when his church would be hosting a healing service. The guest minister, Healing Evangelist Billy Smith, just told me to invite the Holy Spirit to come into my heart and surrender to Him if I want to serve Him. I was to receive the gift of the Holy Spirit in faith. Then he told me to begin to praise God, but not in any language that I know, which included English, French and German. Suddenly, a phrase in an unknown language came audibly from my mouth, and my heart was filled with joy. I repeated the phrase several times and later more words were added. I had received the gift of praying in tongues that is described in God's Word, and I was in awe. From this day on, my desire to read the Bible, my understanding of the passages, and my relationship with Jesus increased tremendously. I couldn't get enough of God and His Word, and was hungering and thirsting for Him more and more each day. I longed to spend time with God and to serve Him in any way I felt called.

I often wrote in my journal about all the great things I was learning and experiencing. The overuse of my right hand began to cause problems, such as numbness in my fingers and wrist. It sometimes hindered me from writing by hand and on the computer. For some reason, during the night, the pain and numbness was often worse. I decided to put into practice what I had been learning about healing prayer, and regularly commanded the numbness and the pain to leave, in the name of Jesus. I spoke to the symptoms of Carpal Tunnel Syndrome in my wrist, *expecting* them to go away. I had learned that, as a born-again believer, the same Holy Spirit who raised Jesus Christ from the dead lives inside of us, and He gives us the power and authority over pain and sickness. With persistent repetition of these prayers, the symptoms finally left and never returned again!

Little by little, I stepped out of my comfort zone and actually began to pray for the sick and for people with various types of pain. I didn't want to just read about it anymore; I wanted to do it. Jesus, the Healer whom I read about in the Bible, was always with me. I was actually very surprised when Jesus began to heal people through me. The first few times I was stunned!

A group of women had been gathering in the home of a local pastor's wife for devotions and prayer. One day, one of the

213

ladies asked for prayer for a cyst that was developing near her ear. For the first time, the group leader asked me to pray and I chose to do it by laying my hands on the cyst and cursing it in the name of Jesus. I commanded it to shrivel up and die. A few days later, I received an e-mail from the woman saying that it did just that!

The second instant healing took place when several of my family members were attending a funeral in North Bay. One of my sisters had been suffering from an ankle injury and it was causing pain and limiting her motion. The ankle had not healed properly since the injury many months earlier. She asked me if I could do something for her. My reply was, "No, I can't, but God can!" I took her ankle into my hand and commanded the bones to align properly, for all ligaments, tendons and muscles to be properly positioned and to function properly, and for all pain to go away, in the name of Jesus. Then I asked her to step down on that foot in faith. My sister stepped down heavily and experienced no pain. She was also able to sit in a position that she could not do previously since her injury. The pain never returned!

In 2007, I gathered a group of like-minded people and began a little healing prayer group with a pastor from The Oasis, a small church in Barrie. Our little Oasis prayer team once prayed for my hypoactive thyroid condition that I had been suffering with for many years. The symptoms I had included severe fatigue during the day, headaches, digestive problems, constipation, hemorrhoids, and weight gain. I also received prayer at the Barrie Healing Rooms for my thyroid problem the first time I ever visited there. That visit was a wonderful experience in itself. On my way home that night, I became filled with faith and loudly stated, "That's it! I received my healing today!" After a week or so, I received a call from my doctor with the results of my latest blood tests. My thyroid hormone levels were now normal! I had taken myself off the medication about a year before that, and I still had my last prescription for Eltroxin in my wallet. I never had to fill it again! With these blood test results, after the prayers, I officially didn't need the medication anymore. However, the medical professionals had always told me that this condition is "irreversible and incurable!" Both my doctors had always said that "it won't go away" and "it won't get better; it can only get worse." Yet God healed my hypothyroidism anyways because He wanted to prove to me, and to others, that He can do anything! I can honestly say that I haven't suffered from *any* headaches, or any of the other symptoms, for many years.

On another occasion, I developed a very swollen, red, hot foot all of a sudden. It became so painful that I called my friend, Anna, to come pray for me. When she arrived, somehow, she knew that it was "gout". I believe it was a word of knowledge that God gave her because she used that knowledge and prayed specifically for the symptoms of that disease to go away. Then she took me to the local hospital for an official diagnosis. After many hours of waiting with the swollen, painful foot, which I had removed from my boot, I was called in to see the emergency doctor. Without having mentioned my friend's revelation, he diagnosed me with "gout", a disease that I had actually never heard of before. He told me that it could be a long-lasting condition, or one that would continually re-appear and go away again. I rebuked that diagnosis. With a prescription in my hand, Anna drove me home, praying over my foot again as she dropped me off late in the night. The next morning, I stepped out of my bed, put full pressure on the foot, and realized that it was completely healed. All the pain and swelling was gone! This was another prescription that I never had to fill because "gout came out!"

During the years that I was researching and learning about healing, I developed many friendships. I suddenly had Christian brothers and sisters all over the place. Many would communicate with me through e-mail letters and share their struggles with me. I was still eager to receive and write letters. Through the leading of the Holy Spirit, somehow, I was able to help them with Scriptures and e-mail prayers. One friend was healed of all kinds of physical and emotional troubles through e-mailed prayers of faith. The letter-writing that I had loved early in my life was continuing through the internet, and God was using this medium to heal the sick and teach others how to pray for the sick.

Connexus Community Church was birthed out of a vision that our pastor from Oro had. He wanted to create a church that unchurched people love to attend. This sounded exciting to me and I wanted to be a part of that. We launched this church in November 2007. That same month, I also became a volunteer at the Barrie Healing Rooms, where I received more training and experience in healing prayer ministry. Both of these environments excited me to no end, and I loved pouring my heart, mind and spirit into them. God was writing a lot of amazing stories and I got to hear many of them. Jesus, the Healer, continued to do wonderful things and my passion was to share what He was doing with others.

Early in 2008, a women's praise and prayer group began to meet regularly in my home. These women were also eager to share God-stories and to hear about what God had been doing in other people's lives. We all loved to let the Holy Spirit lead our gatherings, which focussed on worship, prayer, sharing, and encouraging one another. Many, many prayers were answered over the almost seven years that we were meeting. They included prayers for the salvation of loved ones, healings, forgiveness, protection, provision, and even prolonging life.

In the spring of 2008, I began to write my story of healing in preparation for a testimony that I was to give when I decided to be baptized in my new church, Connexus. While I was writing, I suddenly felt a very sharp hip pain. It lasted longer than it used to and it was even more painful than the pain I had before my surgery. Instantly, I found myself thinking, *How can I write about my healing when I'm feeling all this pain again...?* By this time, I had learned a lot about how Satan attacks us and deceives us. Satan was interfering with the purposes that God had for me. He was trying to keep me from writing the testimony about my positive experiences with healing. I spoke out loud against these thoughts and cast the devil out of my mind. I actually felt and saw the shadow of a wolf-like figure leave my body, and heard a swooshing sound as it left. I rejected and rebuked the pain. Then I prayed to Jesus and the pain left! I continued to write my testimony, which was later recorded on video at my church.

My right (dislocated) hip has never caused me any pain again since then. However, I did have a battle with the devil for my left hip this year. I began to have pain in my left groin and hip joint area just before Christmas 2013. It had been getting progressively worse during Christmas shopping and grocery shopping trips. Once I was in a Walmart store with two of my sisters and a niece. I had to sit on a bench almost the entire time they were in the store because I just couldn't walk. The day before Christmas Eve, I went into our local grocery store, in Angus, and couldn't make it back to my car without help. My neighbour happened to see me and advised me to go to the Emergency Department at the hospital. Reluctantly, I drove myself there and waited many hours to have x-rays and a diagnosis. The x-rays showed inflammation and I was told to see my doctor to arrange for a specialist appointment.

I suffered through the Christmas and New Year's celebrations and visited my doctor in January. She could see the pain that I was experiencing and my range of motion was not good. My Barrie doctor arranged for me to have an MRI but, because they were very booked up in that department, it would have to wait.

In the meantime, I could barely walk. I had to crawl up the stairs in my home and used a cane at times. Many of my friends from the Angus women's prayer group, the volunteers at the Barrie Healing Rooms, and my prayerful friends at Living Hope Fellowship in Angus prayed for healing of my left hip. I knew that God often heals progressively, and my faith was in that.

During this period of time, in January 2014, I was trying to figure out why I had this pain all of a sudden. Was there unconfessed sin in my life? Did I have unforgiveness in my heart? I was working on this book and I still had to write my own story for it. **Was Satan trying to keep me from writing my story again? Did he think I would throw in the towel and not publish this book of God-stories if I had pain in my body?** Many thoughts crossed my mind, but one stood out. I still needed to deal, in my heart, with an issue involving a miscarriage that I had during my first marriage. The unforgiveness towards my former spouse, and towards myself, was lingering. I knew that unhealthy soul ties needed to be broken.

To get help with this, I turned to a woman of God who had been training me in inner healing ministry for several years— my friend, Charlene, the pastor's wife at Living Hope Fellowship. I scheduled a Sozo ministry session with her and included my two best friends, Anna and Joanne. Through these three women, and by the leading and power of the Holy Spirit, I was able to release inner pain that I had carried for decades. My soul and my spirit were freed up of past hurts and pain. **I soon became freer than I had ever been before—even free to dance in worship!**

I had registered for a conference at Catch the Fire, in Toronto for the end of January. I had recently been asked to edit a book about the history of The Toronto Blessing, called, *From Here To The Nations*. It was being released at this conference, and I didn't want to miss it. On the first night, I asked a friend to come with me. Sylvia helped me get in and out of the conference, literally holding me up in her arms. I felt like a real burden to her since I couldn't even make it to the parking lot on the way out. She had to go get my car for me.

On January 25, 2014, the second day of the conference, I drove alone, trusting that my cane would help me get in and out of the building. No one had prayed for me, but during worship that evening, I suddenly realized that I could put pressure on the bad hip. I began to walk on the spot and there was no pain. Later that night, on my way out of the building, I put my faith into practice and eventually lifted up the cane as I walked towards the parking lot. I was fine! There was no pain at all. I began to repeat "Thank you, Jesus!" over and over again, and praised Him all the way to the car. **God had done it again! I was healed during worship. It was His method of healing and His timing.**

The left hip pain did not return. I was completely well and tested myself many times by running up the stairs in my home. However, I still wanted to have the scheduled MRI done to find out if there was anything physically wrong with my left hip. The MRI was scheduled for February 26 at Royal Victoria Hospital in Barrie. Afterwards, I had to go see my family doctor again to get the results. When I arrived, I told the doctor right away that the pain is completely gone and that I've been divinely healed during a night of worship and prayer at a Christian conference. Of course, she was very curious and asked me some detailed questions. She was very willing to listen to my story and told me that she's really happy to hear that I no longer have any pain.

Then we looked at the MRI report together. She actually printed it out and gave it to me. According to the MRI report, my hips were both really bad, which confirmed that I was not making this up. Yet I had no pain in either of the hips! There was evidence of advanced degeneration and tears, chronic joint membrane thickening, trochanteric bursitis, worn protective covering over the bones, a lack of cartilage, and fluid build-up (edema) that generally causes severe pain. I asked my doctor if she would have recommended pain killers. She replied, "Not only would I have prescribed pain killers, but I was going to send you to a specialist for hip replacement surgery!" I confirmed to her that I had absolutely no pain and that surgery would definitely not be necessary. Again the doctor said that she's happy for me, and that I can make another appointment if this should change.

I took the MRI report to another doctor for a second opinion. He also said, "Go see a specialist for hip surgery, Doris," and he even recommended a surgeon for me. When I told him that I have absolutely no pain, and that I was healed completely during worship by the power of God, he couldn't believe it and said, "God cannot heal that!"

"Yes He can; God can do anything!" I proclaimed confidently. The doctor winced, raised his eyes and smiled.

I believe that God has planned good things for all of us to do for Him. One of these is to give Him glory for what He has already done for us. I give Him glory for healing me of several physical and emotional issues.

Over the past ten years, I've learned that walking with God is so much more fulfilling than walking alone. God is still doing miracles!

My family and I have received other miracles from God as well, including several financial miracles, the miracle of marriage restoration, miracles of protection from storms and accidents, miracles of healing, and miracles of salvation. I still love sharing these stories with family and friends in letters, e-mails, blogs and posts, but I will share them with you, dear readers, in another book.

Doris Schuster, Angus, Ontario

Good News for All of Us

No matter what our struggles are today, we can all learn to smile, laugh, forgive, believe, and love again.

We can all know Jesus Christ as our Saviour, the Father as our helper and healer, and the Holy Spirit as our ever-present source of comfort and peace. If you'd like to know how, feel free to contact me by e-mail at Doris@ChristianEditingServices.org.

One Last Thing

If you enjoyed this collection of miracle stories, please search for the book name or its ISBN number 978-0-9940037-0-6 on Amazon.com or Amazon.ca, and share your thoughts by leaving an encouraging review under the heading "Customer Reviews". Your review might prompt someone to begin or deepen their relationship with Jesus as they read the book.

For inspiration and encouragement, visit my video site and Facebook Page.

www.TheGoodNewsVideos.com
www.Facebook.com/TheGoodNewsVideos

For information on editing and proofreading services for Christian publications, stories and memoirs, visit my website.

www.ChristianEditingServices.org

Other Books by this Author

Healing of Body, Mind and Spirit: How God Heals Sickness, Disease, Pain, Addictions and Depression –Kindle Edition

Available at Amazon.com and Amazon.ca

www.ingramcontent.com/pod-product-compliance
Lightning Source LLC
LaVergne TN
LVHW051627080426
835511LV00016B/2210